Resolutely Black

Conversations with Françoise Vergès

Critical South
*The publication of this series was made possible with the
support of the Andrew W. Mellon Foundation*

Nelly Richard, *Eruptions of Memory*
Néstor Perlongher, *Plebeian Prose*
Bolívar Echeverría, *Modernity and "Whiteness"*
Eduardo Grüner, *The Haitian Revolution*
Aimé Césaire, *Resolutely Black*

Resolutely Black

Conversations with Françoise Vergès

Aimé Césaire

Translated by Matthew B. Smith

polity

First published in French as *Nègre je suis, nègre je resterai: Entretiens avec Françoise Vergès*, © Albin Michel, 2005

This English edition © Polity Press, 2020

Excerpt from Aimé Césaire's The Tragedy of King Christophe reproduced by kind permission of Northwestern University Press and Présence Africaine Éditions. Translation copyright © 2015 by Paul Breslin and Rachel Ney. Translation published 2015 by Northwestern University Press. Originally published in French under the title La tragédie du roi Christophe. Copyright © 1963 by Présence Africaine Éditions. All rights reserved.

Polity Press
65 Bridge Street
Cambridge CB2 1UR, UK

Polity Press
101 Station Landing
Suite 300
Medford, MA 02155, USA

ISBN-13: 978-1-5095-3714-3
ISBN-13: 978-1-5095-3715-0 (pb)

A catalogue record for this book is available from the British Library.

Library of Congress Cataloging-in-Publication Data
Names: Césaire, Aimé, interviewer. | Vergès, Françoise, 1952- interviewee. | Smith, Matthew B., translator.
Title: Resolutely black : conversations with Françoise Vergès / Aimé Césaire ; translated by Matthew B. Smith.
Other titles: Nègre je suis, nègre je resterai. English
Description: Cambridge, UK ; Medford, MA : Polity, 2020. | Series: Critical South | Includes bibliographical references and index. | Summary: "Aimé Césaire's work is foundational for colonial and postcolonial thought. In this unique volume, his responses to Françoise Vergès' questions range over the origins of his political activism, the legacies of slavery and colonialism, the question of reparation for slavery and the problems of marrying literature to politics"-- Provided by publisher.
Identifiers: LCCN 2019029720 (print) | LCCN 2019029721 (ebook) | ISBN 9781509537143 (hardback) | ISBN 9781509537150 (paperback) | ISBN 9781509537167 (epub) | ISBN 9781509539307 (pdf)
Subjects: LCSH: Césaire, Aimé--Interviews. | Authors, Martinican--20th century--Interviews. | Negritude (Literary movement) | Postcolonialism.
Classification: LCC PQ3949.C44 Z4613 2020 (print) | LCC PQ3949.C44 (ebook) | DDC 841/.914--dc23
LC record available at https://lccn.loc.gov/2019029720
LC ebook record available at https://lccn.loc.gov/2019029721

Typeset in 11.5 on 15 pt Sabon
by Fakenham Prepress Solutions, Fakenham, Norfolk NR21 8NL
Printed and bound in Great Britain by TJ International Limited

The publisher has used its best endeavours to ensure that the URLs for external websites referred to in this book are correct and active at the time of going to press. However, the publisher has no responsibility for the websites and can make no guarantee that a site will remain live or that the content is or will remain appropriate.

Every effort has been made to trace all copyright holders, but if any have been overlooked the publisher will be pleased to include any necessary credits in any subsequent reprint or edition.

For further information on Polity, visit our website: politybooks.com

Contents

Note on the Translation

Translating race is no easy matter. This is because, at once a social construct and a lived reality, race is experienced differently in different contexts. To be black means something different in France, and in Francophone countries, than it does in the United States and the Anglophone world. This point – as intuitive and commonsensical as it may seem – is far too often lost in translation.

Efforts to overcome these differences linguistically risk oversimplifying the diversity of black experience. Take the English term "black" itself, for instance, which was widely used in France in the 1990s and early 2000s in place of the French term *noir*. Proponents of the English term saw in its use a sense of belonging to a larger, international black community, one that evoked the civil rights movement in the United States, which knows no equivalent in France. But critics saw it as an unnecessary euphemism – why use an English expression when a French one already exists? – and a refusal to acknowledge race openly. *Noir* has since reemerged as the term most frequently used to speak of black experience in France.

But what does it mean to be black in France, or even in French, for that matter? France, casting itself as a color-blind society, officially rejects race as a category and even prohibits the collection of census data according to race. The lack of statistics relating to race, however, does little to hide the brute reality of racism, which proves the extent to which race is very much a category that matters in France. To be black in France, many have argued, is thus "primarily a response to and rejection of anti-black racism."[1] If the English term "black" allowed the French to ignore race, *noir*, many believe, takes a step in openly acknowledging it. Still, the question of whether "black" adequately translates *noir* or *noir* adequately translates "black" remains unsettled.

In these 2004 interviews, Aimé Césaire only occasionally uses the term *noir*. His term, and one that is forever associated with his name, is *nègre* (the title of the French version of this book is *"Nègre je suis, nègre je resterai"*). Césaire wasn't the first to reclaim this term, but he is perhaps responsible for elevating and popularizing its use at a time when both *noir* and *homme de couleur* were both available as relative terms of distinction.[2] Rather than drawing on these mildly "accepted" terms, Césaire deliberately chose a more confrontational approach with the use of *nègre*, a word rejected by many at the time as offensive (the term remains pejorative today). Hence the name "Négritude," a neologism created by Césaire, for the international movement he started with Léopold Sédar Senghor and Léon Gontran Damas, a movement whose goals were twofold: to contest racism and colonialism by cultural means; and to create a collective identity based on a set of shared cultural values and experiences. In Césaire's hands, the term *nègre* is thus double-edged. On the one hand, the appropriation of this once pejorative term is used as a rallying cry; on the other, it is meant to serve as a stark reminder of slavery and colonialism.

In this respect, Césaire's use of this term is not unlike his much-discussed stance on reparations, articulated here in these conversations with Françoise Vergès. Césaire feared reparations could offer France an easy way out of its dark past and troubled present. By paying its due, not only would France be free of guilt, but it would be easier for it to elude accusations of structural racism. Failing to acknowledge the weight of history, acts of racism could be falsely perceived as chance occurrences spontaneously produced by individual actors, rather than part of a deep-rooted historical phenomenon shaping French society on a more fundamental level. Césaire believed France could still be forced to own up to its past and provide aid to countries in need without succumbing to a fantasy of reconciliation. The past, however, would remain – and should remain – irreparable.

Once synonymous with "slave," the term *nègre* prevents one from forgetting the irreparable damage caused by slavery and colonialism. Its range of meaning – from offensive slur to a self-affirming designator – knows no exact equivalent in English. Throughout the history of its use, it aligns with a different set of English terms depending on the period in question. Brent Hayes Edwards suggests that during the interwar period, when Césaire adopted the term, though its function was similar to the "n-word" in English, it was more closely aligned with "black," which was also a derogatory term in the 1920s, whereas "Negro," written with a capital N in the manner of W. E. B. Du Bois, corresponded at that time more to the French term *Noir*. Of course, these are all rough and fleeting correspondences that would continue to shift over the ensuing decades. For a while, *nègre* was most frequently translated as "negro"; now it isn't uncommon to translate it as "black". It goes without saying that neither of these can account for the historical shifts in its meaning.

Thus, any attempt to translate Césaire's use of *nègre* in 2004 would remain approximate, if not misleading. For this reason, I have decided against seeking a single linguistic match for it. At times, I have left it untranslated when I believe it speaks for itself. At others, I offered what I felt was an appropriate translation for a given context while providing the original in square brackets. My hope is that this will allow the reader to gain a sense of the nuance and range of the term as used by Césaire while serving as a reminder of the plurality of black experience and of the history of slavery and colonialism.

Finally, it is worth mentioning that race and gender are often ignored when discussing a translator's approach. This is unfortunate. As a translator who is both white and male, I am aware that my position affords me certain privileges just as it imposes certain limitations on the strategies I can choose from. Césaire's writing has been deftly handled by a wide range of translators, many of whom are black or people of color, and their strategies are by necessity different from mine. I admire these translations and don't see my approach in opposition to theirs. Nor do I think recognizing the race and gender of a translator should be seen as an apology or justification for the linguistic or stylistic choices made. Still, I believe it is important to acknowledge limits and to see them for what they are: an opportunity to recognize difference, to make a certain level of distance felt, rather than as an excuse to speak on the behalf of others. After all, as Césaire reminds us, the specificity of different cultures is often best seen in the gaps that hold them apart.

Matthew B. Smith

Preface

By Françoise Vergès

It may surprise readers that in France, in the early 2000s, Aimé Césaire was barely known and read outside academic circles. To some, his name was synonymous with the French policy of assimilation, which translated into greater dependency and increased inequalities in the larger French Republic. This is due to the role he played in pushing through the law of departmentalization in 1946, which transformed former slave colonies into overseas departments at a time when colonized peoples were fighting for independence. Although I agree with critics of this law, I was nonetheless surprised that Césaire's other works – his *Discourse on Colonialism*, his 1956 letter of resignation from the French Communist Party (a scathing critique of the French left's indifference to race, which still resonates today), his biography of Toussaint

Louverture, his speeches at the National Assembly, where he had always fought French racist and neocolonial policies – was forgotten. To me, Césaire remained a prominent figure of anticolonialism. He was also familiar to me on a more personal level. Both my paternal grandfather and my father worked closely with him, the former having fought with him to end the colonial status of Guadeloupe, Guiana, Martinique, and Réunion, and the latter in the 1970s to counter the French colonial policies that continued to reign in these lands. I had often seen him at political meetings in Paris but we were never close. Shocked by his increasing marginalization in France, I wrote him a letter in July 2004. I brought up his ties to my family and asked if I could interview him. Ten days later, I received a phone call from his assistant. She told me Césaire was surprised I wasn't there yet, of course he was willing to talk to me, and, given his age, I should waste no time.

A few days later, I was on my way to Fort-de-France, Martinique. Over the course of several mornings, we met in his office where he had served as mayor for 56 years. This man, with whom I was talking for the first time on a one-to-one basis, was extremely gracious, at once attentive and aloof, shy and friendly, interested but also absent at times. I handed him a few books. He took an immediate interest in two recently reprinted Greek and Latin classics. He had always loved literature from this period, especially Greek tragedies, and nothing had changed. However, he didn't show too much enthusiasm for the books on history and art. He was quick to ask me exactly what I hoped to achieve and had a hard time believing these interviews would be of interest to anyone. That his writing continued to resonate with people was unthinkable to him, and he was very surprised to hear that the students I had then at Goldsmiths College in London studied his work closely and quoted from it, especially *Discourse on Colonialism* and *Journal of a Homecoming*.[1] I told him about the fervor surrounding his work in the United States and that I had heard experts from around the world – Japan, Germany, and the Anglophone Caribbean – discuss it at length at a conference at New York University. This made him smile. I made it clear that he was known, admired, and respected throughout the world. People valued his opinions, his take on matters. Sure, in France he wasn't the established figure he was elsewhere, but did that surprise him? "No," he told me, nor did he seem concerned to remedy this. Césaire was skeptical, even disdainful, of awards, recognition, glory. He had chosen to live in Martinique, turning down several opportunities that would have granted him more money or a lavish lifestyle. He was happy on his island. He repeated this several times. However, his feelings toward the French Antilles hadn't always been so charitable: "to talk about the history of the Antilles, my desire to leave the Antilles for good, I mean, this place on the margins of history, this unspeakable pit of hunger, misery and oppression."[2] He had both rejected a romanticized fantasy of the tropical islands, which the famous opening of his *Journal of a Homecoming* describes as "the starving Antilles, the Antilles pockmarked with smallpox, the Antilles dynamited with alcohol, run aground in the mud of this bay, in the dust of this town ominously grounded,"[3] and expressed a deep attachment to Martinique, the "geometric center of love and morality," as Michel Leiris put it.[4] Just like Leiris, he sympathized with the people of Martinique, and were it not for this "affective motivation," he wouldn't have had any reason to take an interest in "the fate of the cane field worker over that of the dockers in Rouen."[5] He also experienced, he said, the anxiety of isolation: "I wasn't a calm person ... I had that Antillean anxiety."[6] An anxiety symptomatic of the "unease of a people whose fate is no longer in their own hands, who feel like a mere accessory in a drama of which they should be the protagonist."[7] He expressed this again to me in these terms: "My dear friend, it isn't easy being Antillean. I'm sure it isn't easy being Réunionese, but that's the way it is, and we have to assume this with courage, dignity, and, if need be, pride."

The city shut down at noon, its streets empty and quiet. In La Savane, a large park along the wharf, we saw the headless, paint-smeared statue of Empress Josephine. The French officials had given up on replacing the head, since each time they tried to fix it, the next night it would go missing again. Lining the park's western edge, on Rue de la Liberté, we strolled past the faded glory of the Bibliothèque Schoelcher, the Musée d'Archéologie Précolombienne et Préhistoire de la Martinique and the Pavillon Bougenot, built in the colonial style. Césaire was very proud of his city, especially the neighborhoods he had modernized by bringing in water and electricity and creating a sewage system. Every Thursday afternoon his driver would take him for a ride through the mountains and along the coast. He invited me to join him. He came with his driver to pick me up and brought with him two books: one on the island's flora so that he could name the flowers and plants we'd see; the other a work of philosophy since I had asked him about his influences when he was younger. He had the driver stop on several occasions for me to admire a particular view, plant, or tree. He'd tell me the names of the various *communes* and explain the ties their elected officials had with his party, the Parti Progressiste Martiniquais (PPM). We drove up Mount Pelée, which was draped in fog. He expressed his admiration for this place. People would recognize him and greet him with respect from afar. Césaire didn't come across as someone who would provoke a casual attitude in you. With a distinguished elegance of times past, he wore a suit and tie every day, and no one would dare think you'd ever catch him in a T-shirt and shorts. We drove back down toward the city of Saint-Pierre where he showed me around. The destruction of this city in a matter of minutes on May 8, 1902 from a volcanic eruption at Mount Pelée remains a significant date for Martinique. Historians speak of a death toll of 28,000 – people suffocated, charred, burned alive – a city covered in ash, a boiling sea where those fleeing the lava sought refuge only to drown, an unbearable heat and stench the following days, corpses in the streets and along the port, buildings in ruins. The city known as the "Paris of the Caribbean" for its theaters, its cultural and social life, became a ghost city in no more than a few minutes. This catastrophe robbed the city of its splendor and prestige, which it would never regain. Today it's a small village that forfeited its status as the capital to Fort-de-France after its destruction. Césaire showed me what remained of the theater, then asked his driver to turn down Fonds-Saint-Denis where a kapok tree stood spreading its majestic branches at the juncture of two roads. Its charred trunk was a reminder of its having been a victim of the 1902 volcanic eruption. But, 50 years later, buds appeared and it started to blossom and grow. Césaire often came to admire this tree, which, more than a century old, didn't just survive a catastrophe but, with its new growth, proved nature's indifference to catastrophes. These are the places he liked to visit, letting his mind wander, jotting down lines of poetry, lost in contemplation.

Every morning, between nine and noon, we'd sit down for our interview. He'd tire quickly, due in part to his age but also to the long life he had lived. He had said and written so much, what was there left to explain, justify, defend, argue? "My poetry speaks for me," he said on more than one occasion. But I wanted to talk about his political work, his less "visible" activity, which hadn't received as much attention: his analysis of French colonialism. Although rather surprised by this interest initially, he indulged me and also asked me many questions about Africa. After learning that I went there often, that I knew South Africa quite well, he wanted me to talk more about it. Our conversations were unstructured, at times bewilderingly so. They carried on for a few days but then it became clear it was time to leave. I understood that Césaire had told me everything he had wanted to tell me.

There are many reasons I had wanted to interview him. First of all, I wanted to remind people of the role Césaire played for the generation of women and men responsible for dismantling colonialism, a role I judged too soon forgotten. He was also, as I said, someone I had heard about throughout my childhood. He knew my grandfather, Raymond Vergès, very well, the two of them having worked together to transform the colonies of Martinique, Guadeloupe, Réunion and Guiana into French departments. Then his work as a deputy of Martinique and leader of the Parti Progressiste Martiniquais made him a familiar name around the house and at political gatherings. He was close with other politicians from Réunion and his party collaborated with leftist parties from the overseas departments on initiatives to democratize the political, social, and cultural life of these territories. I was very familiar with two of his texts: *Journal of a Homecoming* and *Discourse on Colonialism*, which I deemed essential reading for understanding decolonization. In short, Césaire was a well-known figure whom I held in great esteem and for whom I had the utmost respect. Once I began talking about my idea to interview Césaire, many people in France, however, claimed to be unfamiliar with his writing and his work. Or they simply thought he had died. I wasn't too surprised. This was symptomatic of France's opinion of the overseas departments, whose culture and history remained poorly understood, evoked only in passing with offhand and vague comments. I wished to interview him because I was struck by

his relevance for our contemporary moment, which
went against popular opinion with its fixation on
Frantz Fanon, Patrick Chamoiseau or Édouard
Glissant, all important writers who should be
appreciated without eclipsing Césaire. In Césaire's
work, being black is a historical phenomenon,
one tied directly to Africa and the diaspora of its
people. It isn't a trait, but a perceived difference
that adds another dimension to one's experience,
which, though neither better nor worse than that
of others, can't ignore the genealogy of forced
slavery, of deportation, of life on the plantation
and the birth of new societies whose memory of
these events is still very much with us.

As the history of slavery and the slave trade
finally emerged as topics of public debate, the time
seemed right to return to the texts and speeches of
a man who had devoted so much of his thinking
to these matters, a man who received a French
public school education but on an island that was
still colonized by former slaveholders, a man who
was later a student in Paris at the École Normale
Supérieure, that temple of the French elite. His
biography of Toussaint Louverture, his plays, his
speeches, and the place Haiti occupies in his work
speak to the importance of this history in his
writing.[8] Césaire brought a fresh perspective to
debates on the slave trade and slavery, calling
attention to the profoundly brutal and inhumane

nature of these practices and deeming their consequences irreparable. In this respect, he stood out from others who were calling for reparations, which he feared could turn an event with innumerable consequences into a tidy sum. Césaire's writing on colonialism also became increasingly relevant in light of other developments in France, such as the law passed in 2005 that required schools to address the benefits of colonization, or the emergence of "Indigènes de la République,"[9] or the reexamination of France's past by a growing body of works and documentaries.

I didn't want to encourage a nostalgic reading of Césaire. Rather, I sought to bring renewed attention to a voice that bore witness to a century, to the fall of colonial empires and to the questions raised by their collapse, to the writing of the history of the "voiceless," to the vanished of the non-European world.

These interviews present a distillation of Césaire's thinking on a variety of issues. He told me several times, "I've said everything," to which I didn't really know how to respond. And then all of a sudden, he'd light up again and read long excerpts from his poems or from one of his plays, or he'd give a lively and detailed response to one of my questions. He had in effect said a lot and, as he liked to recall, he was a poet first. His profoundly original mind, his mental universe shows how he occupied several worlds at once and entertained relations both deeply felt and reimagined with each on a local and global scale. He looked weary, weary from having to explain himself so much over the years and from having been so poorly understood. I could understand this. He'd rather go for a walk on his island, he told me, and see people who didn't ask him to explain himself but were just happy to talk about the weather, or plants, or other mundane matters. One day, after driving all over the island, he took my hand and told me how hard it was to grow old. He was losing control over his own body, he said. I didn't know what to say. Speaking openly and honestly about the body's decline is a taboo he clearly didn't mind breaking. I was taken aback.

This man known throughout the world kindly responded to people's requests and welcomed with the utmost courtesy students, artists, politicians, journalists, and even tourists who came to greet him. And he never forgot to ask about their lives as well, especially Martinicans eager to meet him: the person who waited in front of his office to introduce to him his French-born granddaughter, or the one who crossed paths with him in the street and asked him how he was doing. This man whom Martinicans always called "Papa Césaire" – an expression his friend Michel Leiris rightly judged a relic of African cultures where respect and esteem for a well-considered individual elicited the use of a parental term, which the French, for their part, perceived as a symptom of the backwardness of Antilleans – never cut himself off from the world, but didn't want to be called upon to justify himself. And yet he was kind enough to respond to my questions, which dealt neither with his poetry nor his plays, but rather with more general topics: slavery and reparations, the French Republic and structural racism, the solitude of power.

Conversations

FRANÇOISE VERGÈS: *You've often talked about how happy you were to leave Martinique as a young man. What provoked that feeling?*

AIMÉ CÉSAIRE: You're from Réunion, so it will be easy for you to understand. I'm from Martinique. I went to elementary school in a town called Basse-Pointe. After primary school, I enrolled in the Lycée Schoelcher where I completed my secondary education. It was at that time that I started to *hate* – and I'm not using the word lightly – the Martinican society I grew up in, which was made up of the black *petite bourgeoisie*. I can still see those people, and, at a young age, I was shocked by their deep-seated need to imitate Europeans. They had the same prejudices as them, practiced the same type of superficial elitism, which upset me greatly. Being shy, and even a bit of a recluse, I decided to get away. That world wasn't for me.

My dear sister attended an all-girls high school called the "Colonial Boarding School." She entertained her friends on Saturdays and Sundays in the "downstairs room," which is what we called the living room. I'm sure you're familiar with the layout of colonial homes: on the ground floor was the living room and dining room divided by a hallway and a stairway leading up to the second floor. My sister and her friends were all very nice. Still, their social gatherings downstairs weren't my thing; they made me extremely uncomfortable. I'd seek refuge upstairs.

I found the men from Martinique mild-mannered, superficial, a little snobbish, harboring all the prejudices that "distinguished" black men had at that time. I didn't care at all for that, and I have to say I was thrilled to go to France. Deep down I told myself: "They can't bother me there. I'll be free and I'll read whatever I want."

Going to France offered the promise of freedom, of opportunities, of hope and self-discovery. That's to say, unlike a lot of friends of my generation, I had the constant feeling of being stuck in a small and narrow world, a colonial world. That feeling was with me from the start. I didn't like that Martinique. And once I could leave, I did so without thinking twice. The only thing I had to say was "So long!"

On the boat I was horrified by the idea of socializing with the sort of Martinicans whose sole concern was to dress up and rehearse the rites of their social world on board: Saturday balls, music, nightclubs, all the fashionable activities which made me terribly uncomfortable. Back then the trip lasted between 15 and 20 days. There were balls, entertainment, in many respects a *salon* culture; once again I'd take refuge down in the hold, in a tiny cabin, with a buddy who was leaving to study at a vocational school. I only went out for dinner, then would go back and lock myself in my cabin.

I was really very excited when I got to Le Havre. Once there my friend asked me: "Where are you going to live?" "I don't know," I said, "I'll see. What about you?" "I have my school." The school in question was the École Eyrolles, whose main building is located on Boulevard Saint-Germain. It's still around. My buddy had found a room at a hotel in Cachan. I told him, "I'll come with you. Reserve a room for me." And there I was in Cachan. The following day I took the tramway, which left me at Porte d'Orléans, then I took the metro to Boulevard Saint-Michel before heading to the Lycée Louis-le-Grand on the Rue Saint-Jacques.

I was excited and thought to myself: "I'm finally in Paris. I'm fed up with Martinique! Finally I can be myself!" My history teacher, Eugène Revert, the author of a beautiful book on Martinique and cultural encounters, recommended me to the Lycée. He was a very kind and caring man. He had asked me: "Aimé Césaire, what do you want to do after high school?" He wore a full beard, on which I focused my attention while responding, "I want to do what you do, *Monsieur le Professeur.*" "That's great. If you want to be like me, attend the Lycée Louis-le-Grand so that you can prepare for the entrance exam for the École Normale. I think you'll do quite well." The principal at the Lycée Louis-le-Grand gave me a warm welcome. I signed up for *hypokhâgne*[1] and, leaving the main office, I encountered a rather short man of average stature wearing a gray coat. Right away I knew he was a boarder. He had a string tied around his waist that held an inkwell, an empty inkwell. He came up to me and said: "Hey, newbie, what's your name, where are you from and what are you doing here?" "My name is Aimé Césaire. I'm from Martinique and I just signed up for *hypokhâgne.* You?" "My name is Léopold Sedar Senghor. I'm from Senegal and I'm in *khâgne.*" "Newbie," he embraced me, "you'll be my newbie." All this on my first day at the Lycée Louis-le-Grand! We remained close friends, he in *khâgne* and me in *hypokhâgne.* We saw and talked to each other every day. In his first year Georges Pompidou was in his class and they had become friends – I also met him myself at the time.

Senghor and I would have lively discussions about Africa, the Antilles, colonialism, different civilizations. He loved to talk about Roman and Greek civilizations. He was an impressive Hellenist. In short, we learned a lot from each over time, until one day a fundamental question began to preoccupy us: "Who am I? Who are we? What are we in this white world?" It was a hell of a problem. Then came an ethical question: "What should I do?" This was followed by a metaphysical one: "What can we expect?" We spent a lot of time thinking about these three questions. These discussions had a major impact on the both of us.

We'd talk about the news. This was during the Ethiopian War. We discussed European imperialism and, a little later, the rise of fascism and racism. We quickly took a position, which shaped who we were becoming. These were our principal concerns at the time. Then came the war. I went back to Fort-de-France and was granted a position at the Lycée Schoelcher. Senghor took a job at a *lycée* in France. Back in Paris after the war, and whom do I see? A short man wearing a sort of toga: Senghor was there as a deputy of Senegal just as I was of Martinique. Once again our paths crossed. Our friendship was as strong as ever in spite of our different personalities. He was African and I was Caribbean; he was Catholic, and politically closely aligned with the Mouvement Républicain Populaire.[2] At that time, I was more of a communist or a "communist sympathizer." We never argued, because we had tremendous respect for one another, and we really learned a lot from each other.

FV: *Let's go back to those early years and to that new sense of freedom you were talking about. What were you reading at the time?*

AC: We read the required works, but each of us also had his own particular tastes. Of course, we read the classics – Lamartine, Victor Hugo, or Alfred de Vigny – but they didn't always respond to our concerns. Rimbaud was a major figure for us with his: "*Je suis un nègre.*" We were also reading Claudel and the Surrealists. And, even if we didn't have a lot of money, we'd buy books by contemporary writers.

Two sisters from Martinique, the Nardal sisters, kept a popular *salon*. Senghor went often. I didn't care much for *salons*, but I didn't have anything against them either. I only went once or twice and didn't stay for long. I met a lot of black American writers [*écrivains nègres américains*], Langston Hughes, Claude McKay. These black Americans [*nègres américains*] were a revelation to us. It was no longer enough to read Homer, Virgil, Corneille, Racine, etc. It was much more important for us to seek out another modern civilization, a proud black culture aware of its history and cultural belonging.

They were the first to affirm their identity, whereas in France assimilation was the tendency, the goal even, of many. With Black Americans, though, they were proud to belong to something unique. We constituted our own world. I had a lot of respect for the teachers at the Lycée, but Senghor and I had our own interests as readers.

I also had a friend from Yugoslavia, Petar Guberina, who invited me to Croatia one summer. I remember thinking it looked like the Caribbean coast, and so I asked him one day: "What's the name of this island?" He'd only speak French with me, and he said it was the equivalent of "Martin" in Croatian. So I thought to myself: "What I'm looking at is Martinique!" And that's how, after I purchased a *cahier d'écolier*, or a schoolboy's notebook, I started to write *Cahier d'un retour au pays natal* [*Journal of a Homecoming*]. It wasn't a homecoming in a strict sense, but rather an evocation, on the Dalmatian coast, of my own island.

FV: So this revelation of black identity occurred in Paris with Senghor. There is a lot of work today on the "transcontinentality" of black experience as a result of slavery. The influence of Africa can be charted across several continents and therefore several cultures – you spoke a lot about this at the time. Did this revelation have an immediate impact on your conception of literature?

AC: Reading Martinican poets was like counting on your fingers: once you got to 12, you had your Alexandrine. They wrote cute things, which we call *doudouisme*.[3] Surrealism was a deliberate refusal of this kind of writing, which is why we took an interest in it. It allowed us to do away with reason, with a false sense of culture, and to draw on deeper forces from within. "You see, Léopold, the world is what it is, you get dressed, you put on your suit, you mingle in *salons*, etc. 'My respects, Madame.' But where is the *nègre* in all that? The *nègre* is absent. But it's there, inside you. Dig deeper and you'll find it there, beneath all those layers of education, the *nègre* at your core. You get what I'm saying, *at your core*." That's exactly what I did, and all that writing in Alexandrines, it felt obsolete to us. "They" had done their writing, but *we* would do something else, because we were *nègres*. It's the *nègre* inside us that we were after.

We became interested in indigenous literature, in folk tales. We stood resolute in the position we shared: "*Nègre* I am, *Nègre* I'll always be." The idea was that there was something specific to being African, to being black. But Senghor and I never fell into black racism. I'm my own person and, with white people, there's respect, a mutual respect.

This self-affirmation came about by asking, "who am I?" European civilization was built on the principle of assimilation. But, I'm sorry, you must be yourself first. That's my point of view, which in Martinique shocked many people. I remember a well-dressed young man of some importance, very elitist, who came up to me, offered his hand, and said: "Césaire, I really like you, I really like what you're doing, but I have one problem: why are you always talking about Africa? We're nothing like those people, they're savages, we're something else." And this young man was even "darker" [*plus marron*] than I was! That shows how entrenched the belief in racial hierarchy was. For me, assimilation was alienation, the worst possible thing.

There were in fact two Martiniques. The "civilized" Martinique, a feudalist society of *békés*, *petits bourgeois*, *nègres* and *mulâtres*.[4] And, existing in tandem with this Martinique, in the countryside, there was the peasant with his hoe, working the cane fields, herding his animals, beating his drum, throwing back his liter of rum. This was the more authentic Martinique.

FV: Does the coexistence of these two Martiniques play a role in the malaise you speak so frequently about? Can you talk more about this?

AC: It's there, and I think we can't do anything about it. We're born with it. There's a feeling of unease that comes with being Martinican, or Antillean, which makes sense. Think about the guy taken from Africa, forced into the hull of a ship, shackled, beaten, humiliated, spat on: how could that leave no trace? I am sure it influenced me. I never experienced it personally, but it doesn't matter, there's no doubt I felt the weight of that history.

FV: *Is there a way out of this unease?*

AC: Through intellectual or political pursuits, by caring for one another. We have to understand each other. Racism in Europe and the United States isn't doing much to help, but we have to be aware in our actions, aware that we're dealing with men, therefore brothers, and that we're in this together. We have to know how to help them, and, in order to help them, understand them.

FV: *After World War Two the colonized world was drawn to communism, as it presented itself as a unifying and nonracial ideology. Is that why you joined the French Communist Party?*

AC: Communism was a step forward, and so for me it was the only option. But it became a religion with very serious flaws. I felt out of place among its members. "We" weren't the same as "them." This was their right, they were French; but I felt black [*nègre*], and they couldn't fully understand me. It was a very big mistake on our part to see ourselves as belonging to the French Communist Party. We were members of the Communist Party of Martinique, and we had to work together with the French Communist Party, to show our solidarity, but it wasn't a question of taking orders from the headquarters in Paris.

What I found shocking in communism, and I experienced it firsthand, was its dogmatism, its dueling factions, and, of course, the way matters were handled as a result. The hardliners never saw themselves as part of the problem, never questioned their own actions. I kept a distance, always on guard. It's also true that I tend to keep to myself. Still, even so, I won't be pushed around.

FV: You've often talked about France's struggle to acknowledge differences. In his work on Martinique and Guadeloupe,[5] your friend Michel Leiris described the pervasive racism among French civil servants. Even among the well-intentioned, there was still a stubborn sense of superiority. Do you think this has changed? How do you perceive this problem today?

AC: France does what it can to stay out of trouble. It still can't shake off problems that are tied to its history. Each population of Europe has its own history, and the French mentality is a product of its own history. Look at the British, they also have their own mentality. Go ask a Dominican, or someone from the Bahamas, or Trinidad: "What are you?" "I'm Trinidadian. I'm Dominican." Ask an Antillean: "What are you?" "I'm French." English-speaking Antilleans can't say they are British, "*because nobody can be an Englishman.*" Nobody can be English, unless you are born *in England.*[6] For the British, racism exists alongside a wider conception of human beings and respect for the other, which explains why assimilation wasn't as strong in the British colonies as it was in the French colonies. The French believed in universality and, for them, there was only one civilization: their own. We believed in this too; but this civilization also had a savage and ruthless side. This split runs through all of nineteenth-century France. The Germans, the British, they understood well before the French that *civilization*, in the singular, doesn't exist. Instead, we have *civilizations*. There is a European civilization, an African civilization, an Asian civilization, and each of these civilizations is made up of specific cultures. Clearly, France was far behind in this regard.

Today France is forced to come to terms with cultural differences. But it is forced by history itself. For a long time France continued to call Algeria French. But this was never true and then, one day, France found itself facing the Algeria problem, the

Africa problem. History interfered and changed the order of things, but we had seen all this coming.

I've advocated for the right of independence for a country like Martinique. Not independence itself, since this isn't what the Martinican people want – they know the country has neither the means nor the resources – but it could be sought. We are not independent, but we have *the right of independence*: this means that we can claim it if need be. We have our own specificity, which doesn't prevent us from being friends. There are long-standing ties between us and France. Why risk losing this? I am Martinican, I really like France, which is what it is. We're united in solidarity, but I am from Martinique. That's my problem with the notion of universal civilization. I didn't become someone else. You're you and I'm me. You have your personality, I have mine, and our respect and willingness to help one another should be mutual.

We could start by asking Europeans what ties they have to Europe. When you look closely, you see it's not so simple ... not just with the French and the British, but think about the Serbians and Bulgarians ...

Martinicans are in need of work; they need to produce something. Martinique can't only be devoted to service. This is what we should be focusing on. Currently, we're devoted only to service. We produce nothing. The problem of employment is crucial. Many Martinicans fear being cut off from France, leaving them or the General Counsel to manage all the country's services. That would be a disaster! Martinique, in charge of all those services? It would have to pay all its civil servants. Martinique can't even afford to pay a third of the civil servants who work in the country. In other words, in a few weeks there'd be riots, a revolution.

And yet we can't sit around saying: "France is in control." We have first to take care of ourselves. We have to work, we have to get organized, we have responsibilities towards our country, towards ourselves. I don't believe there are any insurmountable obstacles. Sure, a certain "negroism" has always existed, especially among people of the same class. Just look at Haiti. What was the result of their revolution? It benefitted a small group of people; as for the others … This is the mark of an all-too-human selfishness, of cronyism, of putting one's self or party or clique above everything else. But it is incumbent on us to reach out beyond these limits, to broaden our horizons.

FV: On March 19, 2006, it will be 60 years since the four former slave colonies (Guadeloupe, Guiana, Martinique, Réunion) became departments. You helped introduce this law. You drew a lot of criticism for this, as did other government officials from these colonies, and were accused of favoring assimilation and dependency. Even if that wasn't your intention, the outcome seemed inevitable. Was it a mistake on your part to put too much trust in France?

AC: What was the situation like before that? Complete misery: the sugarcane industry had collapsed, people were abandoning the countryside and flooding into Fort-de-France, setting up camp on any piece of land they could find, living as squatters. What can you do? City officials had a single-minded approach: send the police. As an intellectual I was elected by people that had ideas, needs, and troubles. The Martinican people didn't care about an ideological stance. They wanted social change, an end to their misery.

Under this arrangement you'd become officially French. Okay, if we're French, give us a French salary, give us family allowances, etc. This line of reasoning was impossible to ignore. Vergès, Girard, and I agreed to draft a bill for departmentalization.[7] I was the first one to use the word "departmentalization" rather than "assimilation," in spite of the fact that, for almost a century, many had been campaigning for assimilation.

Never had a law been more popular: by becoming full French citizens, we would have a right to family allowances, paid leave, etc.; even the civil servants were interested in the potential social benefits.

When I introduced this law, my goal was to have these measures recognized and, surprisingly, there was reluctance among government officials, even among the white ones! We wanted to be European. They didn't know how to justify a refusal of our request. They resisted as long as they could, then, grudgingly, little by little, they gave in. But it took us almost ten years to accomplish anything concrete!

I was the committee spokesman. I was thinking, "Here are my people, they're clamoring for peace, food, clothes, etc. What purpose does a philosophical debate serve?" But at the same time I was telling myself, "This solves a short-term problem, but if we continue in this direction, sooner or later another problem no Martinican, Guadeloupean, or Antillean has even considered will have to be dealt with: *the issue of identity*." "Freedom, equality, fraternity," tout these values all you want, but sooner or later you'll have to deal with the issue of identity. What happened to fraternity? Why have we never experienced it? For the precise reason that France never understood the issues tied to identity. If, say, you're a man who is entitled to certain rights and respect, and well I'm a man too, so I'm also entitled to those rights. Respect me. Only then are we brothers. Now we can embrace each other. That's fraternity.

FV: *In May 2001 the French Parliament unanimously passed a law declaring the slave trade and slavery "crimes against humanity." Since then, some groups have been calling for reparations. This debate isn't new. I became aware during the discussions of the Truth and Reconciliation Commission that establishing "truth" in a colonial context marked by violence is far from straightforward, and that the term "reparation" shifts the conversation away from politics towards a moralistic stance with clear-cut victims and persecutors.*

AC: In fact, someone came to talk to me about this and, when the question of reparations was brought up, I responded: "Listen, do what you can. If it works, so much the better, but personally I think it's far-fetched." It would be too easy: "So you were a slave for x number of years a long time ago, therefore we multiply by y: here's your reparation." And then it would be over. For me no act can put an end to it. It's irreparable. It's done. It's history. I can't do anything about it.

Reparation is a matter of interpretation. I know the Western world too well: "All right dear friend, how much? I'll give you half of that to pay off the slave trade. Okay? It's a deal!" Then it's over: they repaired the matter. But for me it's utterly irreparable. I don't really like the term "reparation." It implies that repairing the matter is possible. The West has to do something, it has to provide aid to countries as they develop, help them thrive. It owes us this aid, but I don't believe that a simple check can pay for reparations. It's a question of aid, not a contract. It's purely moral. I believe it is the duty of Western countries to help us.

Again, for me, it's irreparable. The need to help these people to whom so much harm has been done strikes me as obvious and unquestionable. That's my way of thinking about it, not in terms of reparations. Otherwise the reasoning goes like this: "Okay, fine," then "you got paid now leave us the hell alone"; or "this woman's grandfather sold mine; let's go, pay up!"

In the eighteenth century, Europeans realized something: there was an abundance of wealth to be found in people themselves. They invented a new resource, and somehow convinced Africans to sell them people. It was a vile, disgusting business. What kind of reparations can be had? True, we need a word for this, but it is of secondary importance whether it be "reparations" or something else. I think Africa is *morally* entitled to reparations. But let's try to use other terms and avoid looking like a bunch of beggars pleading for reparations for a crime committed two or three centuries ago. Well, now people are going to think I'm against repara- tions; it's not even a debate worth having.

I think Europeans have a responsibility towards us, as they do to all of the less fortunate, but especially to us for all the misfortune they themselves caused. That's what I call reparations, even if the term isn't entirely apt. I think we should help one another, and all the more so when one party is to a certain extent responsible for the misfortune of the other. I don't want this to become a series of trials, indictments, committees, compensation payments, etc. How much would it be? So many different figures have been put forward ... I think we'd even make them look good: there'd be a bill to pay and then it would all be over ... No, this will never be settled. I'd like to think about it in moral terms rather than financial ones.

We can't give in to a sense of victimhood. This isn't an easy task. We've been educated and taught to see the world in a way that leaves us free of responsibility. Have we ever been responsible for ourselves? We've always been the subjugated, the colonized. This has marked us. You went to school, you learned French, you forgot your native language, etc. When people started to write in Creole, when people decided to teach it, the majority of the population wasn't overcome with joy. I often visit schools, I go talk to people, to kids, I really appreciate these exchanges. Recently I asked a woman whom I had just met: "Madame, you just dropped your kids off at school. You know that an incredible measure has just been passed: Creole is going to be taught in school. Are you happy about this?" She responded: "Happy? No, because *si mwen ka vouyé ick mwen lékol* ('if I send my child to school') it's not for him to learn Creole, but French. He's already learning Creole from me at home." I was struck by this. For her it was common sense. And she wasn't wrong. We are complex people, defined by no one thing. It's not a matter of suppressing a part of ourselves.

FV: Let's go back to the question of assimilation. In 1957 when you founded the Parti Progressiste Martiniquais you were advocating for autonomy. The leftist parties from the four overseas departments joined forces on this front, which ultimately led to the "Convention du Morne-Rouge."[8] Let's recall that on the 16, 17, and 18th of August 1971, the official parties and representatives of Réunion, Guiana, Guadeloupe and Martinique convened to solemnly declare: "by virtue of their unique geography, history, ethnic groups, culture and economic interests, the people from the four territories of Réunion, Guiana, Guadeloupe and Martinique constitute national entities, the reality of which is rooted in the consciousness of these people and felt by each of them differently. Consequently, no one has any legal authority over them; it is the peoples themselves who will determine their own fate in a democratic and sovereign manner." Your party signed this agreement. This position was met with strong resistance from the French government, which, as far back as 1963,

had issued an ordinance designed at the outset to
squelch support for the national liberation struggle
in Algeria among civil servants from these territories.
Many civil servants were exiled to France as a result
of this ordinance known as the "Debré Ordinance."
What do you make of these demands – assimilation,
autonomy, independence – today?

AC: On one end you have assimilation; on the
other, independence. If you bring them together,
you go beyond both to reach another position,
which is broader, more humane, and more in line
with our goals. I'm against assimilation, because
my ancestors were not Gauls. I'm for independence.
Like all Martinicans, I believe in independence, but
I'm not sure how much the people of Martinique
really want it. They think independence is for
others; it's not for them for the time being. My own
position is neither pro-independence nor pro-assim-
ilation, but pro-autonomy, which means preserving
our uniqueness, our own institutional practices, our
own ideals, all while belonging to a greater whole.

No need to tell you how unfavorable this "middle
ground" position is: you upset everyone, from both
the left and the right. And they've let me know how
upset they are. It isn't easy being Antillean. I'm
sure it isn't easy being Réunionese, but that's the
way it is, and we have to assume this with courage,
dignity, and, if need be, pride.

I've talked about our sociocultural problems, but in my opinion, our greatest weakness today is economic. The Antillean economy was always a source of misery and inequality, but at least it existed. What can we say about it now? Currently we're a country that doesn't produce anything, but that consumes more and more. We're in a situation of dependence, which we need to get out of.

FV: In Discourse on Colonialism, *you state early on that "Europe is indefensible," "morally, spiritually indefensible." Further on, you suggest colonialism was in part responsible for "the continent's descent into savagery." I'd like to quote from the text, it's a long quote, but I'll explain my reason for quoting it in full in a moment: "[Nazism] is barbarism, but the supreme barbarism, the crowning barbarism that sums up all the daily barbarisms; it is Nazism, yes, but before [the bourgeoisie] were its victims, they were its accomplices; they tolerated that Nazism before it was inflicted on them, they absolved it, shut their eyes to it, legitimized it, because, until then, it had been applied only to non-European peoples."[9] You're well aware that these are very controversial claims, but what I'd like to hear you talk more about is your interpretation of colonialism as "a sickness of Europe." A number of scholars, myself included, have explored the ties between the metropole and its colonies; this line of thinking rejects the notion that the metropole or colony can be studied in isolation, and seeks rather to uncover the exchanges, borrowings, distortions and refusals that define this relationship.*

AC: The colonial mindset hasn't disappeared. Europe was convinced that it was doing a good deed in Africa. This was followed by the brutality and abuse from the Americans. But this colonial attitude wasn't limited to the West: it was no different with the Russians. And the danger is still with us today. In the near future we may see it among the billions of Chinese. That's how history works. China will become the greatest world power.

And then there's humankind. Humans are knowledgeable creatures, but they're driven by power. This power underlies many social structures. Just as each person must control his natural cruelty, states must learn to control their desire to conquer and subjugate. Human beings are what they are. We come to the world and then quickly realize what an odd gift life is. How did religions come about? Imagine early humans in awe of the sea and the sun. They look to the gods for help and protection from this and from that, and there you have the foundation of all religions. For each danger, each threat, another god is invented. A human being's sense of his own weakness and his perpetual search for protection against forces beyond his control, first and foremost against the forces of nature, that's what we need to understand. The principle of hope is bound to this vision of the world. We're fighting against these forces of nature, against ourselves, and this fight is never entirely winnable. The struggle against our own natural tendencies and our collective struggle go hand in hand. One influences the other.

FV: *We've talked a lot about your political work, but you always presented yourself first and foremost as a poet. How were you able to bring these two activities together?*

AC: I don't know how I managed to bring them together. This also surprises me. You can't say I succeeded. Someone recently sent me the Proust Questionnaire and asked me to respond. What questions! It would take a whole book, which is to say a lifetime, to respond. What do I think about men? What do I think about women? What do I think about myself and my character, etc.? Truthfully, I don't know how to respond. I get my bearings and discover myself in my poetry, probably even more so in the most obscure poems ... And who else can discover this but you, you who reads and rereads me, who does me the honor of pursuing me for, dare I say, years? My poetry has all my answers. I like poetry, and I reread my own work, I value it. It's where I am "me."

Poetry is a form of self-revelation. My poetry certainly contains whatever lies deepest inside my self. Otherwise this "self" remains unknown to me. I only encounter it in my poetry, in poetic imagery.

I inhabit a sacred wound
I inhabit imaginary ancestors
I inhabit an obscure desire
I inhabit a long silence
I inhabit an irremediable thirst
I inhabit a one-thousand-year journey
I inhabit an abandoned cult
between bulb and bulbil I inhabit the unexploited
   space
I inhabit not a vein of the basalt
but the rising tide of lava
which runs at full pitch back up the gulch
to burn all the mosques
I accommodate myself as best I can to this avatar
to an absurdly botched version of paradise
– it is worse than hell –
I inhabit from time to time one of my wounds
each minute I change apartments
and all peace frightens me
   whirlwind of fire
   ascidium like none other to hold the dust of
   wandering worlds
   having spat out the volcano my freshwater entrails
   I remain with my loaves of words and my
                 secret minerals
I inhabit thus a vast thought
but mostly prefer to confine myself
to the littlest of my ideas
or I inhabit a magic formula

but only the first few words
the rest forgotten
I inhabit the ice jam
I inhabit the thaw
I inhabit the face of a great disaster
I inhabit the driest udder
Of the most emaciated flank – the lever of these
    clouds –
I inhabit the halo of the Cactaceae
I inhabit a herd of goats pulling on the teat
of the most desolate argan tree
to tell you the truth I no longer know my correct
    address
bathyal or abyssal
I inhabit the hole of an octopus
I fight with the octopus over an octopus hole

    brother don't insist
    a mess of kelp
    clinging like a parasite
        or twining porana-like
    it's all the same
        and let the wave toss
        and let the sun leech
        and let the wind whip
    round hill of my nothingness

    the atmospheric, no historic pressure
    increases immeasurably my plight
    even as it changes with beauty my words[10]

FV: *If a young Martinican asked you what he should read to discover who he is, what would you recommend?*

AC: World culture. We should be interested in everything: Greek, Latin, Shakespeare, French literature from the classical period, the Romantics, etc. Each individual is responsible for finding the right response. None of us is outside of world civilization. It exists, it's there, and we can learn from it or be misled by it. Each individual has to put in the work.

FV: *In your theatrical work, the figure of the rebel, the Promethean figure who defies time and humankind, appears frequently. Do you see yourself in this figure?*

AC: I was always known to speak my mind. I never accepted anything without questioning it first. In class I was always rebellious. I remember one time in particular when I was in primary school. I was sitting next to a good little boy and I asked him: "What are you reading?" He was reading a book: "Our ancestors, the Gauls had blond hair and blue eyes ..." "You fool," I told him, "go take a look at yourself in the mirror!" It wasn't necessarily the most considered response, but there are some things I never accepted, or only endured against my will.

When I talk about unbearable situations, the first thing I think about is the drab rituals of colonial life: "*Monsieur le Gouverneur, Monsieur le Préfet,*

mon Colonel, mon Général, etc." In life there are
things that are hard to bear and, if we are all making
an effort to make a change, it's because we feel the
urgent need for a new civilization. You've heard
this all before, but it's true: we need another world,
another sun, another conception of life. That's
where a collective effort is needed. In recent times
– I'm saying nothing new here – everything philoso-
phers dreamed of ended in utter disappointment.
Communism didn't turn out at all how people
imagined it ... We need to move towards another
world where violence and hate are feared, where we
respect one another, where we realize our potential.

*FV: Haiti occupies an important place in your
work. You wrote an essay on Toussaint Louverture
and you went to Haiti early on in your career – can
you talk about this experience?*

AC: The first time I went there I was still young.
I met many intellectuals, some were very smart,
but they were real bastards. When I visited the
countryside, I'd see the *nègres* with their spades,
working like chained animals and speaking warmly
to me in Creole with a wonderful accent. They
didn't understand French. They were authentic,
but pitiful. How do you bring the world of intellectuals together with this world of peasants, how do
you achieve a real union between them? It would

be simplistic to say the peasants are always right; it's more complicated than that. In *The Tragedy of King Christophe*, I describe the troubles plaguing a man who has to lead a country like Haiti, a very complex country, and this certainly relates to all the Antilles.

I was intrigued by Toussaint Louverture, and immediately I thought about the French Revolution. You have to begin with the French Revolution to get to Toussaint Louverture. They go hand in hand. In my research I didn't find anything on this topic, even in the classic works on the colonial question during the French Revolution. Now, colonialism isn't a single chapter of this history, but rather something fundamental to it. I'm no historian, but I started studying the French Revolution. I did my own research, I wanted to understand what had happened. The French Revolution is plagued by a major problem, but it's brushed aside cavalierly, even by specialists. I'm talking about the problem of colonialism.

I went back to primary sources, and I came up with a very different idea than the one put forth by real historians. I'm a specialist too, you know: I am *nègre*. They have white blood; mine is black [*nègre*]. And we have a very different point of view; naturally I have a different understanding of the French Revolution, a different understanding of Toussaint Louverture, and a different understanding of Haiti. This understanding could be right or wrong, but it's mine.

I see myself in the book on Toussaint Louverture, which, in my opinion, is very honest. I have an old habit of dividing my works into three parts. First, the French Revolution in Haiti. Even the white people rose up. I call this period: "The uprising of the *Grands Blancs*,"[11] because they were defending their own interests. Some Frenchmen fought against this uprising. In need of help, they called on a class of men whose existence was well known but rarely talked about: the mulattos, or the free men of color. This group took control of the movement. Right away it became clear that the group constituted its own social class, and that they were defending the interests of their class. They fought against the *Grands Blancs*, but they spoke *nègre*. So you have two classes: the *Grands Blancs* and the mulattos, neither of which realizes there's another class, which is made up of black slaves from Africa [*esclaves nègres africains*]. For them, it was neither an uprising nor a revolt. It was a revolution. The Haitian Revolution was a Black Revolution [*une révolution nègre*].

So, three stages: the uprising, then the mulatto revolt, which failed, and finally the revolution, when the vast majority of the black population [*population nègre*] made itself heard. This culminates with the arrival of Toussaint Louverture. The problems don't go away after the Revolution, as solutions were never sought for them. There is the problem of class and, underlying this, the problem of race, because class, as can be seen here, often depends on race. The relation between the two isn't clear-cut or straightforward, but I still think race underpins class. After the black rebellion [*la révolte nègre*], a new regime took over, a very Antillean regime: a majority of mulattos filled the top positions in the administration and, over time, the mulatto class never ceded any power. From time to time, black movements [*mouvements nègres*] gained power and ended up as dictatorships.

FV: *The solitude of power felt by leaders of colonial emancipation movements is a recurring theme in your work.*

AC: Indeed, I think this solitude is real. When I went to Haiti, I noticed a great deal of problems. It would have been poor taste to bring them up then, but the color of my skin allowed me to see them. But what could the Haitians do? What were their options? I didn't know. I met some good men, but I felt they were powerless. Their efforts seemed trivial in the face of a terribly complex society and its frequent tragedies. One day in a group setting I met a man who looked shy, very reserved: this man was *Docteur* Duvalier, Papa Doc. He didn't talk politics. He looked like a rather calm intellectual, but in reality he was driven by a terrible ambition. Later on, I saw a real intellectual in Aristide, a very reasonable man, but not at all a leader of men, absolutely not. When he came to Martinique he gave a speech that seemed more like an academic lecture.

In Haiti I saw above all else what shouldn't be done! A country that had supposedly won freedom, won independence, and which I saw more miserable than Martinique, a French colony! Intellectuals devoted themselves to "intellectual" matters: they wrote poems, they took positions on the issue of the day, but they remained cut off from the people. It was tragic, and Martinique could have gone in the same direction.

It was shortly after this experience that I wrote *The Tragedy of King Christophe*. This play also owes much to the trip I took to Cap-Haïtien.[12] Christophe was viewed as a ridiculous figure, a man who spent his time aping the French. There's truth to this, and this is what people focused on, but I'm also a black man [*un nègre*], and this black man [*ce nègre*] could do more than just "ape." This ape was a deep thinker who suffered real anguish; I wanted to find the tragedy behind the ridiculousness. *The Tragedy of King Christophe* isn't a comedy. It's a very real tragedy, because it's ours. What does Christophe do? He sets up a monarchy. He wants to imitate the French king and surrounds himself with dukes, marquises, a whole court. This whole act is a farce, but behind this pageantry, behind the man himself, lies a tragedy that raises very profound questions about cultural encounters. These people use Europe as a model while Europe makes a complete mockery of them. This is no secret.

Here's how I imagined his court – you'd think you're at the King of France's court.

Christophe is wearing the royal coat:

Christophe: Ow! Ow! Who's biting my leg?

It's the king's fool. Hugonin is the king's fool, and he's coming out from under the table.

Hugonin: Bow-wow-wow! I wish to say that I am His Majesty's dog, his pug, his lapdog, his mastiff, his bulldog!

Christophe: A compliment that bites my calf! Go lie down, you spawn of an imbecile!

He is the buffoon, and he is often not far from the truth.

Prézeau: A message, Your Majesty. A letter from London, delivered by way of Sir Alexis Popham.

This man, Wilberforce, is, if you will, the ancestor of Schoelcher, the eighteenth-century Schoelcher. He was a *négrophile*.

Christophe: My noble friend Wilberforce! Felicitations on the anniversary of my coronation. Ha ... he writes that he has enrolled me in several scientific societies, as well as the Bible Society of England! [*Laughter.*] How's that, Archbishop? Can that do any harm? But Wilberforce, you teach me nothing, and you are not the only one to reason thus: "*One does not invent a tree, one plants it! One does not extract its fruits, but allows it to bear them. A nation is not a creation, but rather a gradual ripening, year by year, ring by ring.*" Well, isn't that good! Be prudent! *Sow*, he tells me, *sow the seeds of civilization.* Right. But unfortunately those grow damned slowly. *We must give time due time.*

But we don't have time to wait when it's precisely time that has us by the throat! To entrust the fate of a people to sun, rain, and the seasons, what a strange idea!

Madame Christophe: Christophe!
I am nothing but a poor woman, I
Who served, though I'm now queen,
At the Inn of the Crown!
A crown on my head won't make me anything else
Than the simple woman,
The good black woman [*négresse*], who tells her
    husband:
"Beware!"
Beware, Christophe, of putting the roof of one
    house
On top of another –
It will fall through, or it will be too big.
Christophe, don't demand too much of men,
And too much of yourself!

Isn't that so Martinican? I can almost see the person
I just described. [Césaire continues in his feminine
"Madame Christophe" voice.]

Besides, I'm a mother,
And sometimes when I see you spurring the fiery
Horse of your heart,
My own heart
Falters, and I say to myself:
Let's hope we won't measure
The children's misery by their father's excess!
Our children, Christophe, think of our children.
My God! How will all of this end?

Christophe: I demand too much of men! But not
    enough of black folks [*nègres*], Madame. If there's
    anything that irritates me as much as the talk of
    pro-slavery hacks, it's hearing our philanthropists
    cry, no doubt with the best of intentions, that all
    men are men and that there's no such thing as
    whites and blacks. That's idle thinking, cut off
    from the world, Madame. All men have the same
    rights. That I affirm. But of our common kind,
    some have more responsibilities than others. There
    is the inequality. An inequality of demands, do
    you understand? Who will have us believe that all
    men, I say all, without privilege, without special
    exemption, have known deportation, trafficking,
    slavery, collective debasement to the status of
    beasts, total outrage, enormous insult, which all
    who have suffered it wear, plastered over their
    bodies, their faces: the all-annihilating spit! We
    alone, Madame, you understand, we alone, we
    blacks [*nègres*]! Plunged, then, in the depths of

the ditch! Oh yes, I understand well: in the lowest depths of the ditch. It is there that we cry out; from there we aspire to the air, the light, the sun. And if we want to climb out again, see what demands that lays on us – the foot arching, the muscles straining, teeth that can grip and hold! And the head, oh, the head, capacious and cool. And therefore one must demand more of blacks [*nègres*] than of others: more work, more faith, more enthusiasm, a step, another step, and yet one more step, and to keep what is gained with each step! It's of a resurgence never yet seen that I speak, good sirs, and woe to him whose foot slides back!

Madame Christophe: A king indeed.
Christophe, do you know how, in my little
Wooly head, I think of a king?
I'll tell you! In the midst of savannahs ravaged
By spiteful sun, he's the full and vigorous leaves
Of the great mombin tree, under which
Cattle, thirsting for shadow, take refuge.
But you? But you?
Sometimes I ask myself –
Because you try to do everything,
To control everything – if you aren't instead
The great fig tree that takes all the plants
Growing around it and strangles them!

Christophe: That is called the "Accursed Fig Tree."
Think about it, dear wife!
Ah! I demand too much of blacks [*nègres*]?
... There! Listen! Somewhere in the night, the tam-tam beats.
Somewhere in the night, my people dance. And it's like that every day as well.[13]

Madame Christophe appeals to our common sense. My grandmother talked like that. I wrote based on what I knew from experience. Imagine a woman who lived then and had been a slave. She could have easily felt resigned to her fate and acted accordingly. That is completely understandable. In fact, we're dealing with an ancient tragedy.

Senghor and I thought we had to speak to the people, but how do you address them? I wasn't going to reach the masses through poetry, so I thought: "What if we did theater, if we tackled our problems and staged our history in a way that everyone could understand it?" We were moving away from the conventional history that had been written from its beginnings by white people. I had no illusion about solving anything. I didn't know where we were going, but I knew we had to push forward. Black people [*l'homme nègre*] need to be liberated, but we also have to liberate the liberators. The problem runs deep. It's a problem of self-identity.

FV: You explore this destabilizing effect of power both in The Tragedy of King Christophe *and* A Season in the Congo.

AC: Was my portrayal of Lumumba accepted among Africans? I took some risks. During the Independence celebration, King Baudouin made a speech, then someone spoke up in opposition to the other official speeches. It was Lumumba:

> I, my lord, I think of the forgotten.
> We are those who were dispossessed, struck, mutilated
> – those
> who were addressed as inferiors, whose faces were spat upon.
> Cookboys, chamberboys, laundryboys, we were people of boys,
> a people of 'Yes, Bwana', and whoever doubted that man could
> be not man had only to look at us. Lord, all suffering that can be
> suffered, we have suffered it. All humiliation that can be drunk,
> we've drunk!
> But, comrades, the taste for living, they could not turn it sour in
> the mouth, and we have struggled, with our poor means we have
> struggled for fifty years.
> And look: we have won.
> Our country is now in the hands of her children
> Ours, this sky, this river, these lands.
> Ours, the lake and the forest.
> Ours, Karissimbi, Nyiragongo, Niamuragira, Mikéno, Ehu, mountains
> mounted by the very word of fire.
> Men of Congo, today is a day, big.
> It is the day when the world welcomes among the nations Congo,
> our mother.
> And above all Congo, our child.
> Child of our waking, of our suffering, of our combats.[14]

Such are the illusions of intellectuals. It's a tragedy.
Not necessarily historically accurate but it speaks to
the impatience of the moment. At a later moment
Lumumba speaks up again:

> I hate the time! I hate your "softly and gently"! and
> then, reassure!
> Why reassure! I should have preferred a man who
> made uncomfortable,
> a discomforter! A man who made the people uncom-
> fortable, as I am
> myself, about a future which prepares bad shepherds
> for us![15]

*FV: Do you see anything standing in the way of
solidarity among different black populations?*

AC: That's a very important question, a troubling
one. The fate of Liberia and the Ivory Coast is
frightening. We're protesting colonialism, we're
demanding independence, and we end up fighting
each other. We really have to work towards a united
Africa, which doesn't currently exist. It's horrible,
unbearable. Colonization is in great part responsible for this: it is the root problem. But it's not
the only one, because if there was colonization, it
means Africa had other weaknesses Europeans were
able to exploit when they arrived and took over.

During the period of colonization there were
"tribes." But as black people, we came together

as a whole to win our independence. And now that we're independent, war has broken out; class warfare has turned into race warfare. I think it will take an incredible effort to avoid falling into this trap. Unity has to be reimagined, it has to be built. Africans should at the very least recognize themselves as belonging to the same continent, with a common ideal, and fight together against a common enemy, no longer seeking this enemy within the country but outside it.

Besides, we're dealing with a very rich continent, the envy of the world. The greed for diamonds for instance fueled the war in Sierra Leone. Of course, Europeans haven't failed to deepen these fault lines, but they existed before Europeans interfered. And I've often thought: "Good god, if we had oil in the Antilles, we'd be beside ourselves."

FV: You often talk about a "new humanism."

AC: Let's not make a religion of it. I'd really like to try to understand the problems of Europeans, but they have to understand ours, which are very real. Africans fought to have a country, a nation. But the problem has nothing to do with nationalism in my mind. We have to try to understand humanity and, as far as Africa is concerned, I'm indicating its troubles. I'm trying to discover what caused them in order to find solutions. Martinicans aren't always just having fun, you know! I'm still working on this. When a woman of humble means comes to complain, I might start by taking it bad, then I tell myself I need to understand her, to get to know her particular situation. I look for a solution in spite of everything. It's a matter of one's attitude toward human suffering.

Education can help cultivate this attitude. Unfortunately, the way people were educated, and the way they continue to be educated, is often part of the problem. Where did Hitler learn racism? And wouldn't you say Islamic radicalism is dangerous? I think so. Some forms of Islam have even really hurt Africa. I knew a Kabyle man quite well. He didn't have the highest opinion of people from Algiers, whom he considered colonizers. The Arabs had been ruthless colonizers and slave traders.

And don't think another Antillean will like you just because you're Antillean. I remember Pompidou's response when I asked him: "*Monsieur le Président*, why don't you make a single Martinique–Guadeloupe region?" "Césaire, you don't believe Guadeloupeans like you, do you? It won't work." People have to respect one another, help one another. I have no right to be insensitive to the problems of any *commune* in Guadeloupe. We have to move past this kind of division. Each part of the world should be welcomed into the larger global community.

It's a matter of really believing in humanity and believing in what we call human rights. I always add "Identity" to *Liberty, Equality, Fraternity*. Because, well, we are also due this right. It's what those of us on the left have pushed for. In the overseas regions certain conditions were imposed. I believe the rights of an individual do not depend on where he lives. I think respect for human life must come first.

It doesn't matter who wrote the Declaration of the Rights of Man. What matters is that it exists. Criticizing it as a "Western" creation is simplistic. Who cares? I was always irritated by sectarianism, which I found even in my own party. We have to make this text our own and know how to interpret it correctly. France didn't colonize other countries in the name of human rights. We can tell whatever story we like about what happened: "Look at the unfortunate state of these people. We'd be doing them a service to civilize them." Besides, Europeans believe in a singular *civilization*, while we believe in *civilizations*, in the plural, and in *cultures*. The progressive claim of this declaration is that all people have the same rights, simply because they are human. And these rights, you demand them for yourself and for others.

FV: You're a proponent of what is known as "dialogue among civilizations"?

AC: Yes, it has to be achieved by political and cultural means. We have to learn that each people has its own civilization, culture, history. We have to fight against any policy that legitimizes brutality, war, oppression of the weakest by the strongest. Of utmost importance is humanism, humanity, the respect due to each individual, the respect of human dignity, the right of fulfillment. The way this is talked about of course changes with time, varying with each century and the redrawing of borders, but in the end this is what matters most.

Postface

by Françoise Vergès

A new assessment of these interviews is needed 15 years after their publication in French. Much has changed since. In France, the "race question" has emerged with greater force. Recent events have brought the debate about race and racism to the forefront: the 2005 urban revolts and the creation of the "Parti des Indigènes de la République" that same year; protests against police violence and racist murders; the 2009 general strike in Guadeloupe; the growing body of work from artists, scholars, and novelists on the memories of slavery and colonialism; not to mention the number of books that have appeared on France's colonial policies, on imperialist interventions in Africa, and on the "coloniality" of French republicanism. Indeed, a new light has been shone on France's colonial past and its present manifestations, and people are talking more about structural and state-sponsored racism. The reaction to this has been fierce. Government officials, senators, mayors, intellectuals, journalists, white feminists, and academics have launched an offensive with accusations of antiwhite racism and demands to censor texts and to ban activist-led summer school programs and meetings organized by anticolonial groups and afro-feminists. They have spurred on Islamophobia and targeted figures of the antico-lonial movement, especially women. They claim political antiracism is a threat to republican values to justify their actions. As a result, these interviews with Césaire from 2004 have taken on a new significance and urgency. For this reason, I have updated my original postface to acknowledge what has changed in the intervening years.

It can no longer be said that Césaire is a forgotten figure. These interviews themselves sparked a new interest in his work. A book on Césaire's travels to the USSR has been published; documentaries have been made;[1] articles on his role in the Société Africaine de Culture of which he was a member along with Léopold Sédar Senghor, Richard Wright, and Frantz Fanon have appeared;[2] the role of Suzanne Césaire has been reevaluated; his speeches at the National Assembly have been collected and edited which has led to a better understanding of his political voice. Suddenly, Césaire became fashionable, and political figures, from the right and the left, wanted to be photographed with him. They

thought being seen alongside Césaire would be good
for their own image during a time of intense debate
over the French Republic's coloniality. When, in
2005, Césaire refused to receive Nicolas Sarkozy,
then Minister of the Interior, in order to protest an
article in a 2005 law demanding that the "benefits of
colonization" be taught in schools, the news made
the front page in French papers and news reporters
flew to Martinique. Confronted with the radical
rewriting of a whitewashed colonial history, French
governments (from both the left and the right)
aspired to transform Césaire into a figure of reconciliation and forgiveness. *Journal of a Homecoming*
became Césaire's emblematic text. Once it was read
by a black actor, Jacques Martial, in the Luxembourg
Gardens for the first National Day of the Memories
of the Slave Trade, Slavery and their Abolition on
May 10, 2006, in the presence of the President of the
Republic, it entered the canon as the accepted text
on the memories of slavery and symbolic reparation.
But the image of the French Republic as open
and color-blind was once again belied in a speech
President Nicolas Sarkozy gave at Cheikh Anta Diop
University, Dakar, in 2007, where he declared that
*"the drama of Africa is that the African man has
not entered history."*[3] And yet, when Césaire died
in 2008, Sarkozy ordered a national service and
flew to Fort-de-France for the ceremony. The family
had not wanted him to speak so he was forced to

listen to Pierre Aliker, Césaire's longtime friend, who, quoting Marx, gave a blistering account of colonialism before concluding that Martinicans alone could lead Martinique forward. The transformation of Césaire into an emblem of reconciliation wasn't yet complete. He officially entered the Pantheon on April 6, 2011 after being cast as a gentle old man, a poet who mastered the French language like few before. President Sarkozy declared, "*We are here to say and claim: let Black people from all over enter the great scene of History.*"[4] The great scene of History, which they had not yet entered in 2007, was now open to them and embodied in a building designed for the "great men" of France, yet another celebration of the patriarchal white state. It served to remind people of the undying links between France and its overseas territories, regardless of the crimes committed in the name of France. I was at the Pantheon ceremony. Once again *Journal of a Homecoming* was read, school-children of "all colors" were present, embodying the harmonious "diversity" of France. The entire event was sad, as burials staged as celebrations often are. In an article published on that occasion, I pointed out that Césaire had been a radical critic of the European sense of racial superiority, that he had relentlessly denounced French neocolonialism, and that, already in 1948, he had said France had only answered the demand for equality with a

show of force and police brutality.[5] Yet Césaire is
not without his flaws. The year 1946, for instance,
deserves to be reexamined critically. At that time,
Césaire still argued that only "assimilation will
resolve the problems of the old colonies (Martinique,
Guadeloupe, Guiana, Réunion) and respond to
their needs."[6] Colonialism, he said that same year,
"undermines the very principles of the Republic that
is being built."[7] He never bowed under attack. To
the question "What would you be without France?"
he answered, "A man whose freedom would not
have been taken from him."[8] But he was also mayor
of Fort-de-France and served in the French National
Assembly for decades, and that meant dealing with
governmental policies that led to the worsening
situation in the overseas departments. The idea that
proponents of the 1946 law of departmentalization
should have known it would inevitably lead to
cultural assimilation, systematic repression against
anticolonial movements and parties, censorship,
political corruption, destruction of local indus-
tries, and increased economic dependency, that it
had been a terrible mistake that weighed on, and
would continue to weight on, the overseas societies
and foreclose possibilities of emancipation, swayed
popular opinion about Césaire. He belonged to a
generation who still believed that ethical principles
mattered and who distinguished the Republic from
colonialism. Already in the early 1950s, the law

of departmentalization was seen as a scam and Césaire joined others in calling for a "popular and democratic autonomy," which became the leading policy of his own party – the Parti Progressiste Martiniquais – as well as that of local communist parties.

In other words, Césaire's politics were complex, rooted in what appeared to be a pragmatism that rejected revolutionary utopian aspirations. Did his writings and speeches still deserve to be read in 2004, or even now, in a twenty-first century where neoliberalism and authoritarian regimes reign supreme? One year after Césaire's death, Martinique and Guadeloupe experienced the longest and largest strikes in their history against what Guadeloupeans called *profitasyon* (organized exploitation and impoverishment).[9]

The pacification strategy deployed against radical figures is well known. The State first erases any trace of radicalism and collective struggle, then constructs a discourse that celebrates, as is the case here, the exceptional nature of French republicanism and its inherent ability, given its fundamental values and beliefs, to overcome past discriminations. Though it can be said that the attempt to pacify Césaire has not been very effective, his words continue to be used to support governmental politics. Thus his argument (made in the interviews I conducted) that slavery was irreparable was taken by President

François Hollande to justify the constant refusal to even pronounce the word 'reparation' when evoking colonial slavery. Césaire had, however, explained his argument thus: he feared that, once Europeans gave a symbolic sum of money, they would consider the matter closed, even though the legacies of colonial slavery could be witnessed everywhere, which means that Europe had a debt towards Africa and the diasporas. There had been a similar attempt, long before Césaire, to pacify Frantz Fanon through selective reading. When, in 1998, the French socialist government decided to celebrate the 150th anniversary of the final and definitive abolition of slavery in the French colonies, it followed the suggestion of its event planning committee to promote the occasion with Fanon's words, "I am not the slave of slavery." It meant, according to the government, that the past was the past, that demands for reparations were not justified, and that, thanks to the Republic, the reconciliation of descendants of masters and of slaves had been complete. This was clearly not Fanon's intention: he was more concerned with contesting Europe's repeated attempts to imprison the black man within a narrative frame.

When I reached out to Césaire in 2004, my goal then was to make his political voice heard, which was already present in his theater, his essays, and his speeches. I didn't want to impose a political reading on his poetry. I just wanted to welcome him back into the anticolonial canon. My point was that Césaire could be read outside, or along, the familiar frames of literary criticism, Francophone literature or Négritude. In 2004, I sought to show what Césaire could mean for postcolonial studies, which were not only nearly invisible in France, but also accused of importing US divisive *communautarisme*,[10] or of marginalizing the issue of class, or, more simply, of offering nothing new.

Césaire and Slavery

In 2004, when I discussed slavery in the colonies with Césaire, there was a widespread perception of an orchestrated silence, of a willfully veiled truth. Fifteen years later, it seems France still hasn't fully grasped the effects that centuries of slavery had on its own society, on the societies that suffered under this practice, and on the world at large. Despite the progress attested to by new fields of research, by numerous publications, documentaries, exhibitions; despite the opening of new exhibit halls dedicated to the slave trade and slavery in the colonial era in museums in Nantes, Bordeaux, La Rochelle, Lorient; despite the creation of a museum in Pointe-à-Pitre and the Memorial to the Abolition of Slavery in Nantes; despite the new

Center of Slavery Studies at the Centre National de Recherches Scientifiques (CNRS), the issue of race continues to pose challenges that have yet to be overcome.

It is true that public schools in France focus little on slavery and the slave trade, but in the four former slave colonies – Guadeloupe, Guiana, Martinique, Réunion – many have long advocated for incorporating this history.[11] Since 1983, the abolition of slavery has become an official holiday on the respective days of its enactment; works of history have been published on the topic, and the law of May 2001 declaring the slave trade and slavery crimes against humanity was unanimously passed. None of this was enough to break the perceived silence.

The current marginalization of slavery signals a blind spot in French thought. A blind spot because, how else can one reconcile a narrative that sees slavery as a premodern practice of times past *and* as a foundation of modernity, which is to say, how can one account for its very existence at a time when significant progress was being made in many other arenas (juridical, philosophic, political, cultural, economic)? Addressing this blind spot would require returning to the imperial/colonial project and its relation to the nation. This, in turn, would require a reexamination of the place of "race" at the heart of nationalism. In short, the abolitionist narrative would have to be rewritten. It would start by acknowledging that the abolition of slavery in 1848 wasn't a key turning point, as it is often thought to have been. Indeed, it represented neither a break from the past nor the founding of a new order.

The persistence in its wake of deep socioeconomic disparities, colonial racism, and utter dependency of former slave societies – what we could now call "colonial departments" – in France complicates our understanding of abolition, which stands as both an important date in history and an unkept promise. Abolition became in the national narrative what France had *given* to slaves across the world. In his speech at the Sorbonne on April 27, 1948, Césaire recalled how the order abolishing slavery went almost unnoticed in France.[12] He pointed out that the nineteenth century had witnessed towering figures such as Hugo, Balzac, and Stendhal, which is to say it was a great century for literature and thought, but "at the same time, Africa is being raided and pillaged."[13] Of course, the order of 1848 "made amends and new promises, it recognized the *nègre* who up until then had been the beast of burden in mankind's family."[14] But Schoelcher's work should be seen from "a critical perspective rather than a historical one ... at once vast and inadequate."[15] For, "racism hasn't gone anywhere. It hasn't disappeared. In Europe, it is again awaiting its hour, preying on the weariness and disillusionment of the people. In Africa, it is alive, active, harmful, pitting Muslims against Christians, Jews against Arabs, whites against blacks, and complicating to no end the vexed issue of cultural encounters."[16] Césaire wasn't blinded by his respect for Schoelcher. He found in this universalizing humanist an overestimation of European civilization and a European paternalism.[17] In France, slavery had been "a set of principles, an organized system, propaganda, a way of thinking, a way of feeling and an item of faith all at once."[18] The Republic "had doubts" about abolishing it, and the abolitionists preached, in their paternalistic discourse, "concord and patience." The Republic was willing to restrict political rights since "the *nègres* are not prepared at all for political life," since "the *nègres* are giant children, no more able to understand their rights than they are their responsibilities."[19] As can be seen, Césaire was far from praising Schoelcher and abolition. True, he remained influenced by the pre-World War Two education he received, an approach that still embraced what would later come to be known as "Eurocentrism," and yet, he managed to question the abstract universalism of Europe, to look elsewhere for other models. It was his encounter with Africa that offered him this possibility.

Césaire understood that, in spite of the official narrative of abolition, no single story could do justice to the long history of slavery, which teemed with conflicting memories and stories. Nor could this official narrative offer closure, since the history of slavery continues to influence the way people are represented, which, we know well, has real-life consequences for those concerned.

In France's national narrative, abolition is given pride of place while what preceded and followed it is glossed over. In 1998, no one could miss the image plastered all over by the Socialist government in honor of the 150th anniversary of the abolition of slavery. It showed a group of black and white kids behind the caption: "We were all born in 1848!" France still congratulated itself for the generous gift of freedom it had given to the slaves. Having abolished slavery, the Republic was now free of blame for any past offenses. Never mind the fact that 1848 was also the year Algeria was officially brought under French administration, which effectively stripped inhabitants of their homes and land, or that France sought to curtail the freedom of the newly enfranchised with a series of new measures. Two paintings are emblematic of this revisionist narrative. Each tells a story of reconciliation without reparations. The first is by Marie-Guillemine Benoist (1768–1826), entitled *Portrait d'une Négresse* (1800), later renamed *Portrait d'une Noire* (Portrait of a Black Woman). The painting shows a young black woman, a domestic slave brought to France by her owner, in a pose reminiscent of those struck by high-society women painted by David. In 1998, the portrait was reproduced with her headscarf in the colors of the French flag. Thus, this black woman was shown as another incarnation of "Marianne," that female icon of the nation immortalized by the Third Republic. The other painting, *L'abolition de l'esclavage dans les colonies françaises en 1848*, is by François-Auguste Biard. At the center of the painting two black slaves are shown, unshackled, throwing their arms up in celebration. On the lower quadrant other slaves are kneeling, praising the deputy who, with a tricolor sash wrapped around his waist, stands on a platform with the abolition decree in his hand. His other hand is raised and blends in with the blue, white, and red flag, the symbol of the French Republic. Behind him young sailors stand reminding us of the Navy's presence as an armed force in the colonies, which were managed by the Ministry of the Navy. On the far right side, a former slave woman is kneeling and embracing in gratitude two white women dressed in white. The slaves are scantily clothed, their black bodies entangled to form a compact mass. In the background, coconut trees, farmland, and arid mountains are meant to evoke any sugar island. The centuries-long battle fought by slaves can now be forgotten; both the men and women are reduced to kneeling and grateful victims. Biard's painting conforms to conventional colonial representations. The abolition of slavery is a festive occasion filled only with joy and excitement. The harmonious image of the two communities, who, in spite of their obvious differences, are joined in jubilation, adheres perfectly to the perception the Republic wanted to give of this act: abolition seen as a moment outside of history, emptied of meaning. It wasn't part of the grand narratives that shaped French identity. If accounts of 1848 mention the abolition decree, it is taken as yet another instance of France's illustriousness. But the abolition of slavery in 1848 was not by any means a turning point in French history. This is what Césaire meant when he described it as "vast and inadequate." Social and economic inequality was hardly impacted by this, and the newly enfranchised remained colonial subjects while their masters were compensated for their losses.

Césaire and Colonialism

Césaire confessed it was by chance that he got into politics: "Becoming a politician was less a calling for me than a coincidence. And I say this both with modesty and pride."[20] And yet he came to embody a whole party, the Parti Progressiste Martiniquais, as well as the spirit of the Martinican people whom he represented in the French National Assembly for decades. His name is also tied to the law of departmentalization, which gave the four colonies of France's first stage of colonial expansion – Guadeloupe, Guiana, Martinique, and Réunion – the status of *départements d'outre-mer* (DOM), or overseas departments. These holdovers of an empire that was both prerevolutionary (these lands were colonized in the seventeenth century) and pre-Republican (pre-dating the colonial expansion beginning in 1830 and continuing under the Third Republic) were home to slavery, plantation economies, indentured servitude, forced labor, and colonialism.

When the Committee of the Overseas Territories began debating the proposal of a law that would confer departmental status on Guadeloupe, Martinique, Réunion, and Guiana, there were two camps: one for assimilation and one for autonomy. But neither of these terms indicated what they would come to mean ten years later. In 1946, according to Césaire, "assimilation" meant that "the territories in question be considered an extension of France."[21] Autonomy, on the other hand, meant that the General Counsels would continue to exercise a certain amount of discretion over the budget. But for Césaire and anticolonial groups, the General Counsels were pawns of the plantation owners, whose pockets they'd continue to stuff if they kept their autonomy and were not subject to the French legal system. However, regardless of one's position on this matter, it was clear to them that departmentalization was the sole path to emancipation from the colonial order. Reexamining the positions of the different groups today shows how much the terms of the debate have shifted, just as a careful analysis of the archives reveals an entirely different context that shaped the debate itself. The law was debated before a newly elected Assembly established in the wake of Liberation to create a new constitution for the country. Countless matters were being debated at the time: a new form of governance and a new law for the press; the fate of soldiers from the colonial empire and the treatment of wounded soldiers from the homeland; the return of concentration camp prisoners and survivors; the nationalization of the country's gas and electricity; the role of the colonial empire in the context of decolonization; the rise of North American hegemony; the Cold War; and the resurgence of capitalism in France and across the world. Headlines spoke of the importation of wheat from the Soviet Union, the landing of French troops in "Tonkin," the beginning of the Nuremberg trials, the trials of collaborators, and, above all, the food shortages. Journalists covered riots led by women who ransacked warehouses for their stocks of food, coal, and firewood, which were in dire supply. The demand from the colonies for integration into the *Patrie Française* was buried under all this. Nor was there much talk about what was going on in Indochina, Algeria, or French West Africa. The colonial empire that had filled the Allied ranks with countless soldiers was absent from these conversations. The adoption of the law of departmentalization was hardly covered in the French press. *Le Figaro* and *L'Aurore* make no mention of it; *L'Humanité* makes only a passing reference. The public was enraptured by the constitutional debates but remained indifferent to the jolts suffered by the colonial empire. More serious still, racism and hate showed no signs of letting up. The colonial soldiers demanding repatriation and due pay were being ignored, if not brutally repressed. In response to questions raised about the massacre of the *tirailleurs* at the Thiaroye camp in Senegal, Marius Moutet, Socialist Minister of the Overseas Territories, declared that it was a standard police operation carried out against "soldiers manipulated by the Germans."[22]

The law of departmentalization isn't remembered as an important political event, in spite of its demand for equal rights and its focus on alterity. Césaire expressed as much in an interview given later in his life:

How hard is it to understand that the first step of a people considered for centuries as official citizens of the state, but whose citizenship is given a marginal status, wouldn't be to reject the hollow and debilitated form of their citizenship, but rather to demand that it be fully recognized and respected by the state?[23]

The question raised by the representatives of the "old colonies" could be summed up like this: "You have defended the natural right of equality by declaring 'All men are born free and equal in rights', which you always deemed universal. And yet, besides the constant state of exception upheld in your colonies, in 1848 you officially recognized our equal rights as citizens, without recognizing it in practice. So, if we are your equals but the laws of the state don't apply to us, what does that make you?" In other terms, what can be made of a universal equality that only applies to select individuals? How could you justify this unless you understand equality not as a universal principle but always subject to exceptions? Is it possible to be equal *and* different in the same territory or, in order to be equal and different, must we admit that building a partnership is impossible unless two distinct territories are designated? For Raphaël Confiant, Césaire and his generation were "searching for abstract universals by Western standards, but, as incredible as it may seem to younger generations, they didn't know how to conceive it, due most likely to the unstable and heterogeneous character of a never-satisfied and hybrid Creole culture."[24] According to Confiant, Césaire was always caught between two positions, wavering between denouncing neocolonialism and taking a more moderate approach. He points to an article where Césaire called the leaders of the Front des Antillais et Guyanais pour l'Autonomie (FAGA) (United Front of Antilleans and Guyenese for Autonomy) founded in Paris with, notably, the support of Édouard Glissant,[25] a "pack of Rastignacs foaming at the mouth and supported by two or three over-the-hill political *condottieri*."[26] Denounced by intellectuals and the Communist Party of Martinique for this, Césaire walked back his statement and later testified as a witness at the trial of the Organisation de la Jeunesse Anticolonialiste Martiniquaise (OJAM)[27] (Anticolonial Youth Organization of Martinique), stating that "these are young men who are passionate about France. In a characteristically French spirit, they learned in France to think critically, examining questions from all angles, dissecting them meticulously, weighing all the problems and potential solutions."[28] This wavering between abstract universals and a desire to break with Europe is found throughout Césaire's work. His biography of Toussaint Louverture, for instance, concludes in the following manner: "If this character has a negative side – impossible to avoid given the situation – therein lies the conflict: he was more concerned with conceptualizing the existence of his people based on an abstract universal than seizing on their singularity and giving that singularity a universal value."[29]

The law of departmentalization and its near impossible application reveal once again the Republic's shortcomings in regard to equality. Equality appears more as an ideal, since, each time it is a matter of putting it into practice, new troubles emerge. It is worth noting that the right to social benefits wasn't granted in the overseas departments until the end of the 1990s. The contradictions inherent in France's postwar colonial ambitions come to light in the National Commission's debates. The idea was to organize

> the Union Française, which is to say, to create an organization that would take into account the principles of equality, the great diversity of the colonized populations, commercial interests, new national aspirations, and France's desire to maintain its rank among the major powers. This kind of undertaking is doomed to fail. Sure, maybe you could respect the diversity in the colonies, but then how would a farmer from Auvergne understand he doesn't have the right to an education that conforms to his religion if a farmer from Kabylie does?[30]

Reading the debates today shows how strongly the colonial empire believed it could foster political and economic cooperation as an administrative body with its goodwill alone. But certain conditions were stipulated at the outset. If the union was "agreed upon freely by both parties" and its members granted "all the rights and freedoms essential to all human beings," France, "true to its original mission ... [would guide] the people, whose responsibility it has taken in its own hands, toward the freedom of self-governance and the democratic administration of its internal affairs."[31] The generosity of the first clause was undercut by France's unchanged *mission civilisatrice*. The commission nevertheless set the future prospects of the former slave colonies apart from that of the other colonies. The former's elected officials called for remaining a part of the French Republic and demanded full protection by its laws [*la pleine assimilation à ses lois*, or "legal assimilation"]. The uniqueness of the overseas departments was taken into consideration by government officials, but ultimately used against them: their state of exception wasn't used to address unequal treatment, but to justify it. As Césaire had made clear, "authoritarian regimes that have held power in France always thought these territories should be considered 'lands of exception'."[32] In his speech delivered before the National Constituent Assembly he argued, like those from the anticolonial left before him, for assimilation into the Republic on account of being granted full and equal treatment under its legal system. Assimilation must "be the rule, and derogation, the exception,"[33] Césaire argued. The colonies' inhabitants were subjected to "all the bullying of a ruthless administration," "left defenseless before the greed of a morally depraved capitalism and a reckless administration."[34] Speaking on behalf of these inhabitants, Césaire denounced the benefits the big landowners received from the Republic. Asked to look into the matter, the Finance and Budget Committee insisted the law would be costly. Departmentalization was an expensive undertaking for France at a time when it was trying to rebuild the country. Césaire was outraged that equality was given a price tag, pointing out that tens of thousands of soldiers from the colonies had fought to liberate France. But the colonies had always been the subject of fierce budgetary debates. France was caught between, on the one hand, its *mission civilisatrice* rhetoric of "bringing good to the world at whatever cost," and, on the other, its own economic interests. What were the costs *and* contributions of these colonies? Not much, the government decided, declaring their development impractical. From that point on, it was a matter of enforcing birth control measures and monitoring emigration. Government officials concluded that properly addressing social inequality in the future overseas departments would by costly, since

in order to achieve this goal (equal standard of living), French citizens, taken as a whole, would have

to agree to a 25–30% reduction in their standard
of living for the benefit of our overseas compatriots
… We must therefore take a strong stance against
applying equal standards of living [*l'assimilation des
niveaux de vie*, or "assimilation of living standards"].
And since political, social and economic equality is
neither achievable nor desired, then there is nothing
further to discuss about assimilation.[35]

The law was passed on March 19, 1946, but it
was quickly stripped of its significance. Although
it had been viciously attacked by right-wing groups
before, not until its passing in 1946 had it been
used to bolster their own cultural and economic
positions. Conservatives seized on assimilation as
an excuse to repress the cultural, linguistic, and
religious plurality of the colonies and to shift
attention away from the history of slavery, forced
labor, and colonialism.

In their hands, it became of way of erasing
differences between individuals, of suppressing
distinct markers of identity, but also of establishing a "strategy of segregation and division
based on the assumption that differences exist
between the colonized population and the French
population."[36] As early as 1948, government
officials from the overseas departments protested
the delay in the law's application and continued
to fight inequality. Gradually their battles became
more targeted. In 1953, for instance, Raymond

Vergès called for a National Assembly vote that would "determine which government officials were for or against equal rights, for or against racial discrimination."[37] In the following decades, little was done to improve the social conditions of people who felt increasingly scorned and neglected by the centralized government. Officials held that development in the overseas departments was hindered above all by a high birthrate: women in these countries were having too many children and were therefore responsible for the region's poverty. Social assistance was promised in order to deflect calls for autonomy, but this assistance came with a moral crackdown on sexuality and a policing of black women's bodies. The choice was clear: departmentalization as conceived by the conservative parties or dire poverty. Pierre Messmer, Minister of State for Overseas Departments and Territories, presented this choice in stark terms on June 11, 1971: "It would be a mistake to do away with departmental status if we'd like to hold on to the very important benefits it confers, and I'm not thinking only of material benefits but also of the protection of civil liberties. I have no doubt that any other form of governance would lead to the loss of these liberties, and we'd go either in the direction of Cuba or Haiti."[38] The Minister added that "overpopulation leads to disaffection." While Messmer explicitly stated it wasn't the

government's job "to tell women whether or not
to have kids," two new policies that were put
in place seemed to contradict this. The first was
an aggressive birth control campaign (at a time
when in France birth control was still illegal). The
second was emigration via the program known
as Bumidom (Bureau pour le Développement des
Migrations dans les Départements d'Outre-Mer or
Office for the Management of Migrants from the
Overseas Departments).[39] Beginning in the 1960s,
tens of thousands of people from Guadeloupe,
Guiana, Martinique, and Réunion were sent to
France. Césaire referred to it as a "backdoor
genocide." For some observers, these territories were still colonies in all but name. Michel
Leiris, a longtime friend of Césaire, held such an
opinion. Leiris, who spoke of Césaire's "passion
for humanity," claimed during the trial of 18
young Martinicans in 1963 that "France's policy
enforces cultural assimilation. Youth education in
France fails to consider – or doesn't sufficiently
consider – the cultural and historical conditions
of each locale."[40] Leiris had agreed to testify on
behalf of the young Martinicans belonging to
the OJAM, who were accused of "conspiring
against the authority of the State and attacking the
territorial integrity," charges that were routinely
filed against activists from the overseas departments who contested state policy. Leiris, who

had published a book on the Antilles, called for a better understanding of cultural practices and history: "Before being taught the history of France, young Martinicans, who are almost all the descendants of a mixed race of African slaves brought over by slave traders, should be taught the history of the Antilles."[41] Creole is a language in its own right, he continued, and not a mere patois as French teachers would have us believe. Similar to Césaire, Leiris saw culture as the site of conflict and exchange, of cultural affirmation and creativity.

Césaire spent his entire life questioning what it meant to be born and to live on a land created by colonization and ravaged by slavery, but he sought above all to understand the present-day iterations of this history. He acknowledged having no "feelings of guilt or partisan attachments" concerning the role he played in getting the law of departmentalization passed. He had been clear about the limitations of the law if the cultural dimension wasn't taken into account. "Europe is indefensible," he wrote in the opening pages of *Discourse on Colonialism*, a text that deserves to be reread at a time when a revisionist colonial discourse is again on the rise.[42] To have a deeper understanding of Antillean culture and identity as well as the new humanism he was proposing, one had to first understand the havoc wrought by colonialism, which was destructive for the colonized and the colonizer. Destructive for the colonizer since "colonization works to *decivilize* the colonizer, to *brutalize* him in the true sense of the word, to degrade him, to awaken him to buried instincts, to covetousness, violence, race hatred and moral relativism."[43] Tallying the number of bridges and roads built, as colonial apologists are doing again today, cannot hide the base reality of the colonial world, which was described by colonial writers themselves.[44] *Discourse on Colonialism* is a virulent attack on the inevitable destruction, brutality, and violence wrought by any form of colonialism, which, Césaire suggests, will not end easily.

The limitations of the law of departmentalization reveal a critical blind spot in democracy, which, no matter how much one tries to ignore it, keeps coming back: the notion of race. French thought, which found itself at an impasse as it struggled to accept the intellectual labor of the people it once dominated, faced new pressure under calls for democratization in 1946. Perhaps more surprising is the neglect and marginalization of this moment by scholars and historians. The history of those who stood boldly before the National Constituent Assembly in 1946 is left out of France's grand narrative of decolonization, which is a story of fury and blood, of exile and banishment. The Algerian War furnishes the prototype for this story with its well-known cast of characters: the intellectual *engagé*, the hapless colonizer, the starved colonial subject, the rebel, the reprobate, all set against a Republic attacked for its principles, told and retold as a spectacular stage drama. There is none of this romance in the story of the overseas departments. Only government officials with communist ties, trade unions demanding equal rights, a "republican" vocabulary, etc.

Their demand for equality from the Republic paradoxically excluded these populations from the national narrative. This is because the writing of political history is dictated by precise rules: there must be great orators, romantic heroes, tragic deaths, and scenes where the Republic proves yet again its legitimacy in triumph. In this case, we have only parliamentary debates on electoral fraud, equal pay, milk shortages and the absence of cafeterias in schools, social safety nets and pre- and postnatal care. There's no glory in any of this. The story of assimilation lacks the grandeur and thrill of revolutions. The tale of a compromise sought between two negotiating parties doesn't inspire the same kind of fascination as heroic narratives. Dismantling the colonial system and reclaiming one's dignity amid its ruins offer a more dramatic story than that of fighting for one's dignity through a series of discussions, compromises, and negotiations. However, only a cursory reading of the texts from this period could lead one to accuse this generation of desiring complete assimilation, which is to say, of forsaking their own cultural identity in favor of a French one. Little attention was given to the substance of the 1946 law and, later, the calls for autonomy. This is due to the inability of French thinkers to conceive of the autonomy of its regions in political terms, preferring instead a narrow focus on the notion of "status." Which leads to a single-minded reading: you are either part of France or separate from it, which was how France approached all attempts to redefine this relationship. "We weren't asking to become them; we were asking to be considered equals, and we thought that, after all, if we were to become French citizens, well then that would come with a certain number of rights, and a certain number of disparities would disappear," Césaire clarified again in 1972.[45] The inability to conceive of autonomy wasn't limited to conservatives. In his letter of resignation from the French Communist Party, Césaire excoriated the French Communists for "their obstinate stance on assimilation; their deep-seated chauvinism; their almost fundamental belief – shared with the European bourgeoisie – in the West's unimpeachable superiority; their conviction that Europe's model for growth and progress is the only one possible or desirable, which the rest of the world has no choice but to follow; in short, their faith, rarely openly avowed but nonetheless real, in civilization with a capital C and progress with a capital P (witness their hostility to what they disdainfully refer to as 'cultural relativism'), all of this embodied by the well-educated who, with no instigation, preach their own dogmatism in the name of the party."[46]

"We'd like a partnership, not a ruler. It's their loss if French politicians cannot conceive of an alternative, if the only choice they give is one between subjection and separation," Césaire said almost 20 years later.[47] This raises a political question: can the Republic be decolonized? Can it accept as equals the women and men it colonized? Césaire and backers of the 1946 law wanted to remove the stigma surrounding French citizens who were forgotten or neglected due to their status as descendants of slaves and colonized subjects. Bringing visibility to these citizens would call into question ethno-racial nationalism by revealing the diversity and alterity of French citizens. Discussions of race and racism in France would have to take into account the power struggle between equality and hierarchy, politics and culture, racial domination and racial desire – struggles defined by the history of these territories. Although studies on the colonial empire at times treat the question of race, it is striking to note how frequently the figure of the slave is left out. In most scholarly work on racism, the colonized subject is the main character. However, the slave is the one who is forever bound to a concept of race in the European imaginary: to be a slave is to be black, and to be black is to be tied to slavery and to its abolition, which the Republic prides itself on while doing little to change the equation "black = slave." The republican conception of citizenship is universalist since it depends on relinquishing distinct markers of identity. But this universalism is founded on the notion of reason, and the notion itself is marred by a racial ideology which deems a select group of human beings inherently more rational. Some are therefore *more citizens than others*. The colonized have repeatedly pointed out this contradiction.

A whole generation, however, remains bitter over the law of departmentalization. For Raphaël Confiant, this law weighs like an "original sin" over the Antilles.[48] This position, held by a "son who feels betrayed by his fathers, foremost among them Aimé Césaire" – note the complete absence of women – expresses the despondency and frustration of those who have had to live in a country controlled from the outside, a country where they themselves have little power. Anyone having lived in an overseas department understands this frustration. Time and again the limits of French universalism make themselves felt. How many times do we have to explain we are also wary of *communautarisme*?

Let's recall that we suffered from *communautarisme* in the colonies – in fact one of the first examples of this phenomenon was *colonial communautarisme*, where the "white community" blocked itself off from the people surrounding it and lived as a closed group. Our goal rather is to have our history and culture acknowledged and recognized. Focusing on the relation between equality and alterity – as well as the fear tactics France has regularly deployed for decades by threatening to "let go" of its departments – opens up lines of inquiry that aren't driven by regret. It is a matter of recasting the debate over France's relation with its territories in starker political terms.

Césaire's Relevance Today

Reading Césaire today encourages a reexamination of the notion of race and the role it has played in French thought. In particular, it encourages a reexamination of the place of *le nègre*, to use Césaire's term, in our conception of race. French universalism vehemently rejects any attempt to distinguish groups according to their ethnic and cultural origins. In its very refusal to recognize what makes people different, this universalist position sees itself as charitable. Stripped of distinctions, everyone is equal. But history is stubborn, serving as

a constant reminder that ideals often fall short, and
that more effort should be spent on understanding
what binds individuals together and allows them to
live without conflict. Individuals stripped of their
identity markers do not come together to build
societies. Rather, societies are built by individuals
who define themselves through and by their sense
of belonging. To say that this runs counter to some
social ideal in societies where individuals were
deemed inferior and treated as such is laughable. In
1955, ten years after the equal rights law, Michel
Leiris observed that in Martinique and Guadeloupe
there remained a "colonial-era economy." Leiris
insisted it was the government's job to "ensure that
Martinican and Guadeloupean people of color,
who are now French citizens, are not only equal
by law but also in practice."[49] The challenge for
these people was "to find one's place without
blindly adhering to the cultural norms of a distant
métropole (whose population and living conditions are markedly distinct) nor resorting back to
the antiquated traditions of a culture seen in some
respects as national."[50] Césaire expressed it in
these terms: "There are two ways to be forgotten:
by being isolated into a distinct group or by being
subsumed under the banner of universalism."[51] He
pushed for "invention over imitation" and warned
against "confusing an alliance with domination."[52]
Having experienced colonial paternalism from the

left and the French communists, Césaire understood that new types of relations needed to be
created. His notion of literary "piracy" – urging
writers "to steal from language" – can be applied to
the political arena: stealing the promises of freedom
and equality while ridding them of their ethno-
centric heritage of colonialism and slavery.

When Césaire speaks of a "new humanism,"
he doesn't have in mind, as he himself jokingly
put it, "a new religion." He is more concerned
with confronting and interrogating colonial history
rather than relegating it to the margins. Césaire's
relevancy for the twenty-first century is perhaps
best seen in his *Discourse on Colonialism* and his
notion of the "reverse shock."[53] It is worth citing
the passage in question in full:

> *And then one fine day the bourgeoisie is awakened
> by a terrific reverse shock: the gestapos are busy, the
> prisons fill up, the torturers around the racks invent,
> refine, discuss.*
>
> *People are surprised, they become indignant. They
> say: "How strange! But never mind – it's Nazism, it
> will pass!" And they wait, and they hope; and they
> hide the truth from themselves, that it is barbarism,
> but the supreme barbarism, the crowning barbarism
> that sums up all the daily barbarisms; that it is Nazism,
> yes, but that before they were its victims, they were its
> accomplices; that they tolerated that Nazism before it
> was inflicted on them, that they absolved it, shut their
> eyes to it, legitimized it, because, until then, it had*

*been applied only to non-European peoples; that they
have cultivated that Nazism, that they are responsible
for it, and that before engulfing the whole of Western,
Christian civilization in its reddened waters, it oozes,
seeps, and trickles from every crack.*[54]

According to Césaire, what characterizes the shock
"is not *the crime* in itself, *the crime against man*,
it is not *the humiliation of man as such*, it is the
crime against the white man, the humiliation of
the white man, and the fact that he applied to
Europe colonialist procedures which until then
had been reserved exclusively for the Arabs of
Algeria, the coolies of India, and the blacks [*les
nègres*] of Africa."[55] As studies on structural racism
in French society continue to appear, the notion
of "reverse shock" can be applied to a larger
field of analysis to address the decolonization
of knowledge, institutions, and arts in France.
These questions are already debated among activist
groups, at conferences and in university class-
rooms. Césaire's contribution to this vital process
of decolonization – which remains, as Frantz Fanon
stated, "a historical process,"[56] which is to say,
always an act, a practice, a form of thinking, an
interrogation – is just that: calling attention to
Europe's inevitable descent into savagery, to the
systematic devastation wrought by capitalism, to
the close ties between racism and capitalism. If one
thing is lacking in Césaire's work, it is a discussion

of how women of color are impacted by this system of racialization. At the same time, this shortcoming doesn't stand in the way of women of color filling this gap themselves, and, following the lead of the women's movements in the colonies, many black and brown women in France are doing just that. As for the arts – let's not forget that Césaire, poet and playwright, was passionate about art – it bears repeating that decolonization begins by unmasking the practices and techniques of erasure that are at play in works of art. This is no easy task. A process of unlearning has to happen before learning can take place, and one must ask with unrelenting curiosity "how," "who," "why," and "for whom." In the words of the Algerian-French artist Kader Attia, it is a matter of "empowering yourself and building your own space of resistance and then, as much as possible, connecting it with other spaces of resistance ... And freeing yourself from the yoke of the official national narrative in order to reclaim your story and write it yourself, laying out your vision of things."[57] Learning depends on this process of unlearning, on retraining our damaged senses (seeing, listening, touching, smelling), on reacquainting ourselves with silence.

This turn toward colonial history and its contemporary manifestations is key to decolonizing the arts. Centuries of colonization – both pre- and post-dating slavery – have left us with a whole series

of racist images, taboos, vocabulary. In postwar
France, the moral condemnation of racism created
the fiction that racism was henceforth no more
than a personal opinion, an attitude springing from
a questionable ethical stance. No longer accepting
"race" as a category, however, didn't stand in
the way of a full-flung cultural racism, a *raceless
racism*.[58] This racial ideology has a long history
that has endured in the minds of many: think of
the anti-Semitic representations plaguing Europe
since the medieval period, or the stigmatizing representations of black women and men that began to
spread in the eighteenth century, or of the journals
kept by European travelers where the world was
divided between the civilized and the non-civilized,
or of human zoos, of colonial literature, of the
widespread diffusion of photographic and cinematic
imagery that propped up a racist colonial ideology,
of misogynist and homophobic imagery, which
fed, and continues to feed, widespread beliefs and
practices regarding marginalized populations. "No
one colonizes innocently, no one colonizes with
impunity either; a nation which colonizes, a civilization which justifies colonization – and therefore
force – is already a sick civilization, a civilization that is morally diseased, that irresistibly,
progressing from one consequence to another, one
repudiation to another, calls for its Hitler, I mean
its punishment,"[59] Césaire wrote. And yet, despite

countless works, studies and dissertations on this long history, decolonizing the French cultural castes is still met with strong opposition. Paul Robeson's words would have certainly resonated with Césaire: "Even while demonstrating that he is really an equal (and, strangely, the proof must be superior performance!), the Negro must never appear to be challenging white superiority. Climb up if you can – but don't act 'uppity'. Always show that you are grateful. (Even if what you have gained has been wrested from unwilling powers, be sure to be grateful lest 'they' take it all away.) Above all, do nothing to give them cause to fear you, for then the oppressing hand, which might at times ease up a little, will surely become a fist to knock you down again!"[60]

Works by Aimé Césaire in English

The following list contains only Césaire's most popular works that have appeared in English. For a more extensive list of his work in French, see Kora Véron and Thomas Hale, *Les écrits d'Aimé Césaire*, 2 vols (Honoré Champion, 2013). See also the selected bibliography in *Journal of a Homecoming/ Cahier d'un retour au pays natal* (Duke University Press, 2017).

The Complete Poetry of Aimé Césaire. Translated by A. James Arnold and Clayton Eshleman (Wesleyan University Press, 2017). This work includes a translation of Césaire's most well-known work, *Cahier d'un retour au pays natal*. Two other translations of this work are also worth mentioning: *Journal of a Homecoming/Cahier d'un retour au pays natal*. Translated by N. Gregson Davis, with an editor's preface by F. Abiola Irele (Duke University Press, 2017); and *Return to My Native Land* [1968]. Translated by John Berger and Anna Bostock (Achipelago Books, 2014).

Discourse on Colonialism [1972]. Translated by Joan Pinkham (Monthly Review Press, 2000).

A Season in Congo. Translated by Gayatri Chakravorty Spivak (Seagull, 2010).

A Tempest [1985]. Translated by Richard Miller (Theatre Communications Group, 2002).

The Tragedy of King Christophe. Translated by Paul Breslin and Rachel Ney (Northwestern University Press, 2015).

Notes

Unless otherwise noted, all translations are my own.

Translator's Note

1 See *Black France/France Noire*. Edited by Tricia Keaton, T. Denean Sharpley-Whiting and Tyler Stovall (Duke University Press, 2012), p. 3.
2 Brent Hayes Edwards, *The Practice of Diaspora: Literature, Translation and the Rise of Black Internationalism* (Harvard University Press, 2003). For an enlightening discussion on translating the term "nègre," see especially pp. 17–38. My understanding of the history of these terms is greatly indebted to Edwards' work.

Preface

1 *Discourse on Colonialism* (1972). Translated by Joan Pinkham (Monthly Review Press, 2000); *Journal of a*

Homecoming. Translated by N. Gregson Davis (Duke University Press, 2017). Anglophone readers are fortunate to be able to choose from three widely available translations of Césaire's seminal work *Cahier d'un retour au pays natal.* The 1968 translation by John Berger and Anna Bostock – *Return to My Native Land,* reissued by Archipelago Books in 2014 – has been complemented by two recent translations: a bilingual edition translated by Clayton Eshleman and A. James Arnold (*Notebook of a Return to the Native Land,* in *The Complete Poetry of Aimé Césaire* (Wesleyan University Press, 2017)) and, appearing at the same time, N. Gregson Davis's translation, cited above. All three have much to recommend them, but Davis's bilingual edition seemed to me to offer the most nuanced reading of Césaire's poem. For a comparison of these three translations, see David B. Hobbs, "At the Living Heart: Translating Aimé Césaire," *The Nation,* July 3, 2018. https://www.thenation.com/article/at-the-living-heart/

2 Quoted in Daniel Guérin, *Les Antilles décolonisées* (Présence Africaine, 1956), p. 8.

3 *Journal of a Homecoming,* p. 77.

4 Michel Leiris, 30 octobre 1949, in *Journal: 1922–1989.* Edited by Jean Jamin (Gallimard, 1992, p. 473).

5 Ibid.

6 See his 2003 interview with K. Konaré and A. Kwaté in *Césaire et Nous. Une rencontre entre l'Afrique et les Amériques au xixe siècle* (Cauris Éditions, 2004), p. 11.

7 Aimé Césaire, "Pour la transformation de la Martinique en région dans le cadre d'une Union française fédérée," Speech Delivered at the Constitutive Congress of the *Parti Progressiste Martiniquais,* March 22, 1958 (author's archives).

8 Aimé Césaire, *Toussaint Louverture* (Présence Africaine, 1962); *The Tragedy of King Christophe.* Translated by Paul Breslin and Rachel Ney (Northwestern University Press, 2015); *Victor Schœlcher et l'abolition de l'esclavage* (Éditions Le Capucin, 2004) (reprinted from *Esclavage et colonisation,* PUF, 1948).

9 *Les Indigènes de la République* began as an anti-discriminatory movement in 2005 that viewed France's colonial history as the source of its ongoing problems with discrimination, which became part of a larger national discussion after riots erupted in the Parisian *banlieues* in 2006. It later became its own political party, *Parti des Indigènes de la République* (PIR), which is still active today. *Translator's note.*

Conversations

1 *Hypokhâgne* is the name for the first year of studies at the *Classes préparatoires aux grandes écoles* in France, whose aim is to prepare students for the entrance competition for the École Normale Supérieure, a "temple for the French elite" (see Postface). The second and final year is called *khâgne. Translator's note.*
2 The Mouvement Républicain Populaire, or MRP ("Popular Republican Movement") was a Christian democratic political party in France during the postwar period. *Translator's Note.*
3 *Doudouisme* is named after the term for a child's comfort blanket, *doudou.* As the name suggests, this writing from the Antilles provided a comfortable image of Caribbean culture by reinforcing the exoticizing stereotypes of the colonial imagination. *Translator's note.*
4 *Béké, nègre,* and *mulâtre* correspond in general to *white, black,* and *mixed-race,* respectively. In addition to being indicators of race, these terms also carry strong overtones of class and profession. *Les békés,* for example, or "white creoles," are descendants of European settlers from the colonial period who are still considered by many as the ruling class in Martinique. *Translator's note.*
5 Michel Leiris, *Contacts de civilisations en Martinique et en Guadeloupe* (1955) (Gallimard, 1987).
6 In English in the original.

7 Raymond Vergès, from Réunion, and Rosan Girard, from Guadeloupe, were both deputies of their respective countries. Together with Aimé Césaire, they put forth the bill that led to the end of the colonial status of the four colonies. *Author's note.*

8 This was a political convention in the Morne-Rouge region in Martinique that took place over the course of three days in August 1971. The result of this meeting was the recognition of the failure of departmentalization and the need for political autonomy of the four overseas territories. *Translator's note.*

9 *Discourse on Colonialism* (1972). Translated by Joan Pinkham (Monthly Review Press, 2000), p. 36. *Translation modified.*

10 "Lagoonal Calendar" translated by Carrie Noland. *Voices of Negritude in Modernist Print: Aesthetic Subjectivity, Diaspora, and the Lyric Regime* (Columbia University Press, 2015), pp. 247–8. Although Noland's translation of this poem is a little harder to find than Eshelman's and Arnold's (see *The Complete Poetry of Aimé Césaire*), it is a much more precise and compelling rendering.

11 *Grands Blancs* is the name used to refer to white owners of large plantation companies. *Author's note.*

12 Cap-Haïtien is the site of the former capital of Santo Domingo, located on the island's north side, and was the capital of King Christophe's kingdom. Christophe participated in the uprising alongside Toussaint Louverture that led to the Revolution. Appointed general in 1802, in 1806 he organized a *coup d'état* against Dessalines, who had proclaimed himself Emperor Jacques I of Haiti. Christophe ruled the northern part of the island (the south was in the hands of Alexandre Pétion), first as elected president, then as king, under the name Henri I. He created a noble class, and had the Sans Souci Palace and La Ferrière Fortress built, which Césaire was to visit. Christophe committed suicide in 1820 during mass in a church he had had built. *Author's note.*

13 Aimé Césaire, *The Tragedy of King Christophe*. Translated by Paul Breslin and Rachel Ney (Northwestern University Press, 2015), pp. 35–8.
14 *A Season in the Congo*. Translated by Gayatri Chakravorty Spivak (Seagull Books, 2010), pp. 29–30.
15 Ibid., pp. 130–1.

Postface

1 "Aimé Césaire, un nègre fondamental," written by François Fèvre, directed by Laurent Hasse and Laurent Chevallier, 2007; "Césaire et moi," directed by Isabelle Simeoni and Fabrice Gardel, 2018; "Aimé Césaire et les révoltes du monde," directed by Jérôme-Cécil Auffret and Françoise Vergès, 2013; "Aimé Césaire, le prix de la liberté," directed by Félix Olivier, 2017.
2 Constantin Katsakioris, "L'union soviétique et les intellectuels africains," *Cahiers du monde russe*, 47/1–2, January 1, 2006, available at: http://journals.openedition.org/monderusse/9589
3 *Jeune Afrique*, October 12, 2012.
4 "Césaire: entrée symbolique au Panthéon," *Le Figaro*, April 6, 2011.
5 Françoise Vergès, "Célébré au Panthéon, Aimé Césaire demeure un rebelle irrécupérable," *Le Monde*, April 5, 2011.
6 Aimé Césaire, *Écrits politiques. Discours à l'Assemblée nationale, 1945–1983* (Jean-Michel Place, 2013), p. 33.
7 Ibid., p. 40.
8 Ibid., p. 77.
9 I was invited by Richard Samuel, the Guadeloupean official in charge of the public consultation, to serve as an "expert." I went to Réunion and witnessed how much people wanted to have their wishes, desires, demands, and aspirations heard by the government. The entire process was frustrating and depressing: technocratic vocabulary

imposing its language, white men. In Guadeloupe, the Liyannaj Kont Pwofitasyon (LKP) ("Stand Up against Exploitation"), the platform of organizations and unions led by Éklie Domota, refused to participate. They were right. The entire exercise was a scam to which I unfortunately lent my presence.

10 This term is often associated with American-style identity politics, which some in France see as a sort of cultural and racial factionalism that threatens national unity. *Translator's note.*

11 See the careful analysis of textbooks and curricula in the report issued by the Committee for the Memory of Slavery, entitled *Mémoires de la traite négrière, de l'esclavage et de leurs abolitions* (La Découverte, 2005); Décret, *JO*, no. 83-1003, November 23, 1983, p. 3407.

12 Aimé Césaire, *Victor Schœlcher et l'abolition de l'esclavage* (Éditions Le Capucin, 2004), p. 65.

13 Ibid.

14 Ibid., p. 73.

15 Ibid., p. 75.

16 Ibid., p. 70.

17 See his *Discours du 21 juillet 1951, à Fort-de-France*, in Césaire, *Victor Schœlcher*, p. 86.

18 Césaire, *Victor Schœlcher*, p. 19.

19 Ibid., p. 41.

20 Interview in *Le Monde*, December 6, 1981.

21 Archives of National Constituent Assembly, Commission des Territoires d'Outre-Mer, March 6, 1946. Quoted in Françoise Vergès (ed.), *La Loi du 19 mars 1946. Les débats à l'Assemblée Constituante* (CCT, 1996), p. 44.

22 Ibid., p. 11.

23 Quoted in Guérin, *Les Antilles décolonisées* (Présence Africaine, 1956), p. 10.

24 Raphaël Confiant, *Aimé Césaire, Une traversée paradoxale du siècle* (Stock, 1993), p. 61. For a considered analysis of Césaire's political choices, see also Gary Wilder, *Freedom Time: Negritude, Decolonization and the Future of the World* (Duke University Press, 2015) and *The French*

Imperial Nation-State: Negritude and Colonial Humanism between the Two World Wars (Chicago University Press, 2005); Roger Touson and Simonne Henry-Valmore, *Aimé Césaire, le nègre inconsolé* (Syros, 1993).

25 Hirota Satoshi recounts that, "during the Second Congress of Black Writers and Artists in 1959 in Rome, Édouard Glissant shared with the deputy-poet Aimé Césaire his plan to found the *Front uni des Antillais et Guiyanais pour la revendication de l'autonomie* [FAGA]. Albert Béville and Frantz Fanon were there during this whole exchange. They chimed in and voiced their support for Glissant. But, in spite of his initial agreement, the Negritude poet distanced himself from his fellow countrymen. That was one of the first instances when the two Martinican poets showed clear ideological differences. The Third Congress of the *Association générale des étudiants Martiniquais*, or AGEM [General Association of Martinican Students] was held in Paris on December 27–30, 1959. At a time of heightened emotions due to the bloody repression in Martinique, this conference represents a turning point in the group's ideology. The main topic was 'Antillian-Guianese Unity for a Change of Status.' On April 22 and 23, 1961, at the Hôtel Moderne de la Place de la République, the foundational meeting for the *Front des Antilles et de la Guyane pour l'autonomie* kicked off. Close to 700 people were in attendance to show their support for this United Front. Over the course of two days, intellectuals, representatives of different political parties and student associations discussed the status of the overseas departments as well as the problem and future of colonized peoples throughout the world." (https://edouardglissant.world/lieux/front-antillo-guyanais/, January 28, 2018). The organization was dissolved on July 22, 1961.

26 Confiant, *Aimé Césaire*, p. 206.

27 See the film directed by Camille Mauduech, "La Martinique aux Martiniquais, l'affaire de l'OJAM," 2012.

28 Confiant, *Aimé Césaire*, p. 208.

29 Aimé Césaire, *Toussaint Louverture. La Révolution française et le problème colonial* (Présence africaine, 1981), p. 344.

30 Jacques Bardoux, deputy of the Farmer's Group, quoted in Vergès, *La Loi du 19 mars 1946*, p. 20.

31 Ibid., p. 12.

32 Ibid., p. 72.

33 Ibid., p. 77.

34 Ibid., p. 80.

35 Pierre-Henri Teitgen commenting on the special powers requested by Guy Mollet, quoted in Guérin, *Les Antilles décolonisées*, p. 12.

36 I am indebted here to the analysis of Benjamin Stora, "Passé colonial et représentations françaises de la guerre d'Algérie: le masque de l'universalisme républicain." Presented at the XVIᵉ Conference of the International Association of Political Science, Berlin, August 1994.

37 Annals of the National Assembly, Archives of the National Assembly, Meeting, July 2, 1953.

38 *Le Monde*, June 11, 1971, quoted in Lilyan Kesteloot and Barthélemy Kotchy, *Comprendre Aimé Césaire. L'homme et l'œuvre* (Présence Africaine, 1993), p. 182.

39 The Bureau pour le Développement des Migrations dans les Départements d'Outre-Mer, or Bumidom, was a government office created in 1961 that was responsible for managing the emigration process for people leaving the overseas departments to come to metropolitan France. In 1981, it was replaced by the Agence Nationale pour l'Insertation et la Protection des Travailleurs d'Outre-mers (ANT), or National Agency for the Integration and Protection of Overseas Workers, renamed in 1992 Agence de l'Outre-Mer pour la Mobilité (LADOM), or Oversea Agency for Mobility. *Translator's note.*

40 Daniel Guérin and Michel Leiris, "Les Antilles. Département ou colonie?," *Alithéa*, May 1964, no. 3, pp. 182–6, at p. 183.

41 Ibid., p. 185.

42 *Discourse on Colonialism* (1972). Translated by Joan Pinkham (Monthly Review Press, 2000), p. 32.

43 Ibid., p. 35.

44 See Jacques Weber's edited volume, *Littérature et histoire coloniale* (Les Indes savantes, 2005).

45 Aimé Césaire, Press Conference, University of Laval, Québec, 1972, in Kesteloot and Kotchy, *Comprendre Aimé Césaire*, p. 185

46 Letter to Maurice Thorez, Publication of the Parti Progressiste Martiniquais, undated (author's archives).

47 Aimé Césaire, Press Conference, University of Laval, in Kesteloot and Kotchy, *Comprendre Aimé Césaire*, p. 189.

48 Confiant, *Aimé Césaire*, p. 32.

49 Michel Leiris, *Contacts de civilisation en Martinique et en Guadeloupe* (Gallimard/UNESCO, 1955), p. 10. Leiris had received research funding from the Minister of National Education for the centenary of the 1848 Revolution. His stay lasted from July 26 to November 13, 1948, during which he met Césaire and other intellectuals. The goal of his trip, he explained, was to carry out a "critical analysis of the means established in the French Antilles to integrate non-European peoples into the national community," p. 9.

50 Ibid., p. 113.

51 Aimé Césaire, *Lettre à Maurice Thorez. Discours à la Maison du Sport*, Fort-de-France, Parti Progressiste Martiniquais, *c.* 1956, p. 21 (author's archives).

52 Ibid., pp. 21 and 15, respectively.

53 On this subject, see Michael Rothberg's brilliant analysis of the notion of "reverse shock" in his *Multidirectional Memory: Remembering the Holocaust in the Age of Decolonization* (Stanford University Press, 2009).

54 *Discourse on Colonialism* (1972). Translated by Joan Pinkham (Monthly Review Press, 2000), p. 36.

55 Ibid.

56 See Frantz Fanon, "On Violence," in *The Wretched of the Earth*. Translated by Richard Philcox (Grove Press, 2004), pp. 1–52.

57 https://www.lofficiel.com/art/kader-attia-macval-palais-de-tokyo

58 On the development of raceless racism, see Étienne Balibar and Immanuel Wallerstein, *Race, Class, Nation: Ambiguous Identities* (1991) (Verso, 2011).

59 *Discourse on Colonialism* (1972). Translated by Joan Pinkham (Monthly Review Press, 2000), p. 39.

60 Quoted in Jim Sparrow, *No Way but This: In Search of Paul Robeson* (Scribe Publications, 2017), p. 36.